I0539887

SANITARY AND SOCIAL LECTURES AND ESSAYS

SPECIAL LARGE PRINT EDITION
with easy-to-read text

Charles Kingsley

ſerenity
Publishers, LLC

ROCKVILLE, MARYLAND
2013

ISBN: 978-1-61242-827-7

NOTE

Serenity Publishers can custom create classic texts in large print

We can create new titles with text/margins to your specifications

Add your notes and create the book as you want it

Combine different classic texts in one volume

Produce an edition with a special introduction or an afterword

Add your footnotes

Visit **www.SerenityPublishers.com** &
www.ArcManor.com

or email **chandi@serenitypublishers.com**

Published by Serenity Publishers
An Arc Manor Company
P. O. Box 10339
Rockville, MD 20849-0339
www.SerenityPublishers.com

Printed in the United States of America/United Kingdom

CONTENTS

WOMAN'S WORK IN A COUNTRY PARISH [1]

I have been asked to speak a few words to you on a lady's work in a country parish. I shall confine myself rather to principles than to details; and the first principle which I would impress on you is, that we must all be just before we are generous. I must, indeed, speak plainly on this point. A woman's first duties are to her own family, her own servants. Be not deceived: if anyone cannot rule her own household, she cannot rule the Church of God. If anyone cannot sympathise with the servants with whom she is in contact all day long, she will not really sympathise with the poor whom she sees once a week. I know the temptation not to believe this is very great. It seems so much easier to women to do something for the poor, than for their own ladies' maids, and housemaids, and cooks. And why? Because they can treat the poor as *things:* but they *must* treat their servants as persons. A lady can go into a poor cottage, lay down the law to the inhabitants, reprove them for sins to

---

1   This lecture was one of a series of "Lectures to Ladies," given in London in 1855, at the Needlewoman's Institution.

which she has never been tempted; tell them how to set things right, which, if she had the doing of them, I fear she would do even more confusedly and slovenly than they. She can give them a tract, as she might a pill; and then a shilling, as something sweet after the medicine; and she can go out again and see no more of them till her benevolent mood recurs: but with the servants it is not so. She knows their characters; and, what is more, they know hers; they know her private history, her little weaknesses. Perhaps she is a little in their power, and she is shy with them. She is afraid of beginning a good work with them, because, if she does, she will be forced to carry it out; and it cannot be cold, dry, perfunctory, official: it must be hearty, living, loving, personal. She must make them her friends; and perhaps she is afraid of doing that, for fear they should take liberties, as it is called—which they very probably will do, unless she keeps up a very high standard of self-restraint and earnestness in her own life—and that involves a great deal of trouble, and so she is tempted, when she wishes to do good, to fall back on the poor people in the cottages outside, who, as she fancies, know nothing about her, and will never find out whether or not she acts up to the rules which she lays down for them. Be not deceived, I say, in this case also. Fancy not that they know nothing about you. There is nothing secret which shall not be made manifest; and what you do in the closet is surely proclaimed (and often with exaggeration enough and to spare) on the house-top. These poor folks at your gate know well enough, through servants and trades-men, what you are, how you treat your servants, how you pay your bills, what sort of temper you have; and they form a shrewd, hard estimate of your character, in the light of which they view all that you do and say to them; and believe me, that if you wish to do any real good to them, you must begin by doing good to those who lie still nearer to you than them. And believe me, too, that if you shrink from a hearty pa-triarchal sympathy with your own servants, because it would require too much personal human intercourse with them, you are like a man who, finding that he had not powder enough to fire off a pocket-pistol, should try to better matters by using the same quanti-ty of ammunition in an eighty-four pound gun. For it is this human friendship, trust, affection, which is the very thing you have to employ towards the poor, and to call up in them. Clubs, societies, alms, lending li-braries are but dead machinery, needful, perhaps, but, like the iron tube without the powder, unable to send the bullet forth one single inch; dead and useless lum-ber, without humanity; without the smile of the lip, the light of the eye, the tenderness of the voice, which makes the poor woman feel that a soul is speaking to her soul, a heart yearning after her heart; that she is not merely a *thing* to be improved, but a sister to be made conscious of the divine bond of her sisterhood, and taught what she means when she repeats in her Creed, "I believe in the communion of saints." This is my text, and my key-note—whatever else I may say to-day is but a carrying out into details of the one question, How may you go to these poor creatures as woman to woman?

Your next duties are to your husband's or father's servants and workmen. It is said that a clergyman's wife ought to consider the parish as *her* flock as well as her husband's. It may be so: I believe the dogma to be much overstated just now. But of a landlord's, or employer's wife (I am inclined to say, too, of an officer's wife), such a doctrine is absolutely true, and cannot be overstated. A large proportion, therefore, of your parish work will be to influence the men of your family to do their duty by their dependants. You wish to cure the evils under which they labour. The greater proportion of these are in the hands of your men relatives. It is a mockery, for instance, in you to visit the fever-stricken cottage, while your husband leaves it in a state which breeds that fever. Your business is to go to him and say, *"Here is a wrong; right it!"* This, as many a beautiful Middle Age legend tells us, has been woman's function in all uncivilised times; not merely to melt man's heart to pity, but to awaken it to duty. But the man must see that the woman is in earnest: that if he will not repair the wrong by justice, she will, if possible (as in those old legends), by self-sacrifice. Be sure this method will conquer. Do but say: "If you will not new-roof that cottage, if you will not make that drain, I will. I will not buy a new dress till it is done; I will sell the horse you gave me, pawn the bracelet you gave me, but the thing shall be done."

Let him see, I say, that you are in earnest, and he will feel that your message is a divine one, which he must obey for very shame and weariness, if for nothing else. This is in my eyes the second part of a woman's parish work. I entreat you to bear it in mind when you hear, as I trust you will, lectures in this place upon that *sanitary reform*, without which all efforts for the bettering of the masses are in my eyes not only useless, but hypocritical.

I will suppose, then, that you are fulfilling home duties in self-restraint, and love, and in the fear of God. I will suppose that you are using all your woman's influence on the mind of your family, in behalf of tenants and workmen; and I tell you frankly, that unless this be first done, you are paying a tithe of mint and anise, and neglecting common righteousness and mercy. But you wish to do more: you wish for personal contact with the poor round you, for the pure enjoyment of doing good to them with your own hands. How are you to set about it? First, there are clubs—clothing-clubs, shoe-clubs, maternal-clubs; all very good in their way. But do not fancy that they are the greater part of your parish work. Rather watch and fear lest they become substitutes for your real parish work; lest the bustle and amusement of playing at shopkeeper, or penny-collector, once a week, should blind you to your real power—your real treasure, by spending which you become all the richer. What you have to do is to ennoble and purify the *womanhood* of these poor women; to make them better daughters, sisters, wives, mothers: and all the clubs in the world will not do that; they are but palliatives of a great evil, which they do not touch; cloaks for almsgiving, clumsy means of eking out insufficient wages; at best, kindly contrivances for tricking into temporary thriftiness a degraded and reckless peasantry. Miserable, miserable state of things! out of which the longer I live I see less hope of escape, saving by an emigration, which shall drain us of all the healthy, strong, and brave among the lower classes, and leave us, as a just punishment for our sins, only the cripple, the drunkard, and the beggar.

Yet these clubs *must* be carried on. They make life a little more possible; they lighten hearts, if but for a moment; they inculcate habits of order and self-restraint, which may be useful when the poor man finds himself in Canada or Australia. And it is a cruel utilitarianism to refuse to palliate the symptoms because you cannot cure the disease itself. You will give opiates to the suffering, who must die nevertheless. Let him slip into his grave at least as painlessly as you can. And so you must use these charitable societies, remembering all along what a fearful and humbling sign the necessity for them is of the diseased state of this England, as the sportula and universal almsgiving was of the decadence of Rome.

However, the work has to be done; and such as it is, it is especially fitted for young unmarried ladies. It requires no deep knowledge of human nature. It makes them aware of the amount of suffering and struggling which lies around them, without bringing them in that most undesirable contact with the coarser forms of evil which house-visitation must do; and the mere business habits of accuracy and patience to which it compels them, are a valuable practical schooling for them themselves in after-life. It is tiresome and un-sentimental drudgery, no doubt; but perhaps all the better training on that account. And, after all, the magic of sweetness, grace, and courtesy may shed a hallowing and humanising light over the meanest work, and the smile of God may spread from lip to lip, and the light of God from eye to eye, even between the giver and receiver of a penny, till the poor woman goes home, saying in her heart, "I have not only found the life of my hand—I have found a sister for time and for eternity."

But there is another field of parish usefulness which I cannot recommend too earnestly, and that is, the school. There you may work as hard as you will, and how you will—provided you do it in a lov-ing, hearty, cheerful, *human* way, playful and yet ear-nest; two qualities which, when they exist in their highest power, are sure to go together. I say, how you will. I am no pedant about schools; I care less what is taught than how it is taught. The merest rudiments of Christianity, the merest rudiments of popular in-struction, are enough, provided they be given by lips which speak as if they believed what they said, and with a look which shows real love for the pupil. Man-ner is everything—matter a secondary consideration;

for in matter, brain only speaks to brain; in manner, soul speaks to soul. If you want Christ's lost-lambs really to believe that He died for them, you will do it better by one little act of interest and affection, than by making them learn by heart whole commentaries—even as Miss Nightingale has preached Christ crucified to those poor soldiers by acts of plain outward drudgery, more livingly, and really, and convincingly than she could have done by ten thousand sermons, and made many a noble lad, I doubt not, say in his heart, for the first time in his wild life, "I can believe now that Christ died for me, for here is one whom He has taught to die for me in like wise." And this blessed effect of school-work, remember, is not confined to the children. It goes home with them to the parents. The child becomes an object of interest and respect in their eyes, when they see it an object of interest and respect in yours. If they see that you look on it as an awful and glorious being, the child of God, the co-heir of Christ, they learn gradually to look on it in the same light. They become afraid and ashamed (and it is a noble fear and shame) to do and say before it what they used to do and say; afraid to ill-use it. It becomes to them a mysterious visitor (sad that it should be so, but true as sad) from a higher and purer sphere, who must be treated with something of courtesy and respect, who must even be asked to teach them something of its new knowledge; and the school, and the ladies' interest in the school, become to the degraded parents a living sign that those children's angels do indeed behold the face of their Father which is in heaven.

Now, there is one thing in school-work which I wish to press on you; and that is, that you should not confine your work to the girls; but bestow it as freely on those who need it more, and who (paradoxical as it may seem) will respond to it more deeply and freely— *the boys.* I am not going to enter into the reasons *why.* I only entreat you to believe me, that by helping to educate the boys, or even (when old enough), by taking a class (as I have seen done with admirable effect) of grown-up lads, you may influence for ever not only the happiness of your pupils, but of the girls whom they will hereafter marry. It will be a boon to your own sex as well as to ours to teach them courtesy, self-restraint, reverence for physical weakness, admiration of tenderness and gentleness; and it is one which only a lady can bestow. Only by being accustomed in youth to converse with ladies, will the boy learn to treat hereafter his sweetheart or his wife like a gentleman. There is a latent chivalry, doubt it not, in the heart of every untutored clod; if it dies out in him (as it too often does), it were better for him, I often think, if he had never been born: but the only talisman which will keep it alive, much more develop it into its fulness, is friendly and revering intercourse with women of higher rank than himself, between whom and him there is a great and yet a blessed gulf fixed.

I have left to the last the most important subject of all; and that is, what is called "visiting the poor." It is an endless subject; if you go into details, you might write volumes on it. All I can do this afternoon is to keep to my own key-note, and say, Visit whom, when, and where you will; but let your visits be those of woman to woman. Consider to whom you go—to poor souls whose life, compared with yours, is one long malaise of body, and soul, and spirit—and do as you would be done by; instead of reproving and fault-finding, encourage. In God's name, encourage. They scramble through life's rocks, bogs, and thornbrakes, clumsily enough, and have many a fall, poor things! But why, in the name of a God of love and justice, is the lady, rolling along the smooth turnpike-road in her comfortable carriage, to be calling out all day long to the poor soul who drags on beside her over hedge and ditch, moss and moor, bare-footed and weary-hearted, with half-a-dozen children at her back: "You ought not to have fallen here; and it was very cowardly to lie down there; and it was your duty, as a mother, to have helped that child through the puddle; while, as for sleeping under that bush, it is most imprudent and inadmissible?" Why not encourage her, praise her, cheer her on her weary way by loving words, and keep your reproofs for yourself—even your advice; for *she* does get on her way, after all, where *you* could not travel a step forward; and she knows what she is about perhaps better than you do, and what she has to en-dure, and what God thinks of her life-journey. The heart knoweth its own bitterness, and a stranger in-termeddleth not with its joy. But do not be a stranger to her. Be a sister to her. I do not ask you to take her up in your carriage. You cannot; perhaps it is good for her that you cannot. It is good sometimes for Lazarus that he is not fit to sit at Dives's feast—good for him that he should receive his evil things in this life, and be comforted in the life to come. All I ask is, do to the poor soul as you would have her do to you in her place. Do not interrupt and vex her (for she is busy enough already) with remedies which she does not understand, for troubles which you do not understand. But speak comfortably to her, and say: "I cannot feel *with* you, but I do feel *for* you: I should enjoy helping you, but I do not know how—tell me. Tell me where the yoke galls; tell me why that forehead is grown old before its time: I may be able to ease the burden, to put fresh light into the eyes; and if not, still tell me, simply because I am a woman, and know the relief of pouring out my own soul into loving ears, even though in the depths of despair." Yes, paradoxical as it may seem, I am convinced that the only way to help these poor women humanly and really, is to begin by confessing to them that you do not know how to help them; to humble yourself to them, and to ask their counsel for the good of themselves and of their neighbours, instead of coming proudly to them, with nostrums ready compounded, as if a doctor should be so confident in his own knowledge of books and medicine as to give physic before asking the patient's symptoms.

Therefore, I entreat you to bear in mind (for without this all visiting of the poor will be utterly void and useless), that you must regulate your conduct to them, and in their houses, even to the most minute particulars, by the very same rules which apply to persons of your own class. Never let any woman say of you (thought fatal to all confidence, all influence!): "Yes, it is all very kind: but she does not behave to me as she would to one of her own quality." Piety, earnestness, affectionateness, eloquence—all may be nullified and stultified by simply keeping a poor woman standing in her own cottage while you sit, or entering her house, even at her own request, while she is at meals. She may decline to sit; she may beg you to come in, all the more reason for refusing utterly to obey her, because it shows that that very inward gulf between you and her still exists in her mind, which it is the object of your visit to bridge over. If you know her to be in trouble, touch on that trouble as you would with a lady. Woman's heart is alike in all ranks, and the deepest sorrow is the one of which she speaks the last and least. We should not like anyone—no, not an angel from heaven, to come into our houses without knocking at the door, and say: "I hear you are very ill off—I will lend you a hundred pounds. I think you are very careless of money, I will take your accounts into my own hands;" and still less again: "Your son is a very bad, profligate, disgraceful fellow, who is not fit to be mentioned; I intend to take him out of your hands and reform him myself." Neither do the poor like such unceremonious mercy, such untender tenderness, benevolence at horse-play, mistaking kicks for caresses. They do not like it, they will not respond to it, save in parishes which have been demoralised by officious and indiscriminate benevolence, and where the last remaining virtues of the poor, savage self-help and independence, have been exchanged (as I have too often seen them exchanged) for organised begging and hypocrisy.

I would that you would all read, ladies, and consider well the traits of an opposite character which have just come to light (to me, I am ashamed to say, for the first time) in the Biography of Sidney Smith. The love and admiration which that truly brave and loving man won from everyone, rich or poor, with whom he came in contact, seems to me to have arisen from the one fact, that without perhaps having any such conscious intention, he treated rich and poor, his own servants and the noblemen his guests, alike, and *alike* courteously, considerately, cheerfully, affectionately—so leaving a blessing and reaping a blessing wheresoever he went.

Approach, then, these poor women as sisters, and you will be able gradually to reverse the hard saying of which I made use just now: "Do not apply remedies which they do not understand, to diseases which you do not understand." Learn lovingly and patiently (aye, and reverently, for there is that in every human being which deserves reverence, and must be reverenced if we wish to understand it)—learn, I say, to understand their troubles, and by that time they will have learnt to understand your remedies, and they will appreciate them. For you *have* remedies. I do not undervalue your position. No man on earth is less inclined to undervalue the real power of wealth, rank, accomplishments, manners—even physical beauty. All are talents from God, and I give God thanks when I see them possessed by any human being; for I know that they, too, can be used in His service, and brought to bear on the true emancipation of woman—her emancipation, not from man (as some foolish persons fancy), but from the devil, "the slanderer and divider" who divides her from man, and makes her live a life-long tragedy, which goes on in more cottages than in palaces—a vie à part, a vie incomprise—a life made up half of ill-usage, half of unnecessary, self-willed, self-conceited martyrdom, instead of being (as God intended) half of the human universe, a helpmeet for man, and the one bright spot which makes this world endurable. Towards making her that, and so realising the primeval mission by every cottage hearth, each of you can do something; for each of you have some talent, power, knowledge, attraction between soul and soul, which the cottager's wife has not, and by which you may draw her to you with (as the prophet says) human bonds and the cords of love: but she must be drawn by them alone, or your work is nothing, and though you give the treasures of Ind, they are valueless equally to her and to Christ; for they are not given in His name, which is that boundless tenderness, consideration, patience, self-sacrifice, by which even the cup of cold water is a precious offering—as God grant your labour may be!

THE SCIENCE OF HEALTH [2]

Whether the British race is improving or degenerating? What, if it seem probably degenerating, are the causes of so great an evil? How they can be, if not destroyed, at least arrested? These are questions worthy attention, not of statesmen only and medical men, but of every father and mother in these isles. I shall say somewhat about them in this Essay; and say it in a form which ought to be intelligible to fathers and mothers of every class, from the highest to the lowest, in hopes of convincing some of them at least that the science of health, now so utterly neglected in our curriculum of so-called education, ought to be taught—the rudiments of it at least—in every school, college, and university.

We talk of our hardy forefathers; and rightly. But they were hardy, just as the savage is usually hardy, because none but the hardy lived. They may have been able to say of themselves—as they do in a State paper of 1515, now well known through the pages

---

2   The substance of this Essay was a lecture on Physical Education, given at the Midland Institute, Birmingham, in 1872.

of Mr. Froude: "What comyn folk of all the world may compare with the comyns of England, in riches, freedom, liberty, welfare, and all prosperity? What comyn folk is so mighty, and so strong in the felde, as the comyns of England?" They may have been fed on "great shins of beef," till they became, as Benvenuto Cellini calls them, "the English wild beasts." But they increased in numbers slowly, if at all, for centuries. Those terrible laws of natural selection, which issue in "the survival of the fittest," cleared off the less fit, in every generation, principally by infantile disease, often by wholesale famine and pestilence; and left, on the whole, only those of the strongest constitutions to perpetuate a hardy, valiant, and enterprising race.

At last came a sudden and unprecedented change. In the first years of this century, steam and commerce produced an enormous increase in the population. Millions of fresh human beings found employment, married, brought up children who found employment in their turn, and learnt to live more or less civilised lives. An event, doubtless, for which God is to be thanked. A quite new phase of humanity, bringing with it new vices and new dangers: but bringing, also, not merely new comforts, but new noblenesses, new generosities, new conceptions of duty, and of how that duty should be done. It is childish to regret the old times, when our soot-grimed manufacturing districts were green with lonely farms. To murmur at the transformation would be, I believe, to murmur at the will of Him without whom not a sparrow falls to the ground.

The old order changeth, yielding place to the new,
And God fulfils himself in many ways,
Lest one good custom should corrupt the world.

Our duty is, instead of longing for the good old custom, to take care of the good new custom, lest it should corrupt the world in like wise. And it may do so thus:

The rapid increase of population during the first half of this century began at a moment when the British stock was specially exhausted; namely, about the end of the long French war. There may have been periods of exhaustion, at least in England, before that. There may have been one here, as there seems to have been on the Continent, after the Crusades; and another after the Wars of the Roses. There was certainly a period of severe exhaustion at the end of Elizabeth's reign, due both to the long Spanish and Irish wars and to the terrible endemics introduced from abroad; an exhaustion which may have caused, in part, the national weakness which hung upon us during the reign of the Stuarts. But after none of these did the survival of the less fit suddenly become more easy; or the discovery of steam power, and the acquisition of a colonial empire, create at once a fresh demand for human beings and a fresh supply of food for them. Britain, at the beginning of the nineteenth century, was in an altogether new social situation,

At the beginning of the great French war; and, indeed, ever since the beginning of the war with Spain in 1739—often snubbed as the "war about Jenkins's ear"—but which was, as I hold, one of the most just, as it was one of the most popular, of all our wars; after, too, the once famous "forty fine harvests" of the eighteenth century, the British people, from the gentleman who led to the soldier or sailor who followed, were one of the mightiest and most capable races which the world has ever seen, comparable best to the old Roman, at his mightiest and most capable period. That, at least, their works testify. They created—as far as man can be said to create anything—the British Empire. They won for us our colonies, our commerce, the mastery of the seas of all the world. But at what a cost!

Their bones are scattered far and wide,
By mount, and stream, and sea.

Year after year, till the final triumph of Waterloo, not battle only, but worse destroyers than shot and shell—fatigue and disease—had been carrying off our stoutest, ablest, healthiest young men, each of whom represented, alas! a maiden left unmarried at home, or married, in default, to a less able man. The strongest went to the war; each who fell left a weaklier man to continue the race; while of those who did not fall, too many returned with tainted and weakened constitutions, to injure, it may be, generations yet unborn. The middle classes, being mostly engaged in peaceful pursuits, suffered less of this decimation of their finest young men; and to that fact I attribute much of their increasing preponderance, social, political, and intellectual, to this very day. One cannot walk the streets of any of our great commercial cities without seeing plenty of men, young and middle-aged, whose whole bearing and stature shows that the manly vigour of our middle class is anything but exhausted. In Liverpool, especially, I have been much struck not only with the vigorous countenance, but with the bodily size of the mercantile men on 'Change. But it must be remembered always, first, that these men are the very elite of their class; the cleverest men; the men capable of doing most work; and next, that they are, almost all of them, from the great merchant who has his villa out of town, and perhaps his moor in the Highlands, down to the sturdy young volunteer who serves in the haberdasher's shop, country-bred men; and that the question is, not what they are like now, but what their children and grandchildren, especially the fine young volunteer's, will be like? A very serious question I hold that to be, and for this reason.

War is, without doubt, the most hideous physical curse which fallen man inflicts upon himself; and for this simple reason, that it reverses the very laws of nature, and is more cruel even than pestilence. For instead of issuing in the survival of the fittest, it issues in the survival of the less fit: and therefore, if protracted, must deteriorate generations yet unborn. And yet a peace such as we now enjoy, prosperous, civilised, humane, is fraught, though to a less degree, with the very same ill effect.

In the first place, tens of thousands—who knows it not?—lead sedentary and unwholesome lives, stooping, asphyxiated, employing as small a fraction of their bodies as of their minds. And all this in dwellings, workshops, what not?—the influences, the very atmosphere of which tend not to health, but to unhealth, and to drunkenness as a solace under the feeling of unhealth and depression. And that such a life must tell upon their offspring, and if their offspring grow up under similar circumstances, upon their offspring's offspring, till a whole population may become permanently degraded, who does not know? For who that walks through the by-streets of any great city does not see? Moreover, and this is one of the most fearful problems with which modern civilisation has to deal—we interfere with natural selection by our conscientious care of life, as surely as does war itself. If war kills the most fit to live, we save alive those who—looking at them from a merely physical point of view—are most fit to die. Everything which makes it more easy to live; every sanitary reform, prevention of pestilence, medical discovery, amelioration of climate, drainage of soil, improvement in dwelling-houses, workhouses, gaols; every reformatory school, every hospital, every cure of drunkenness, every influence, in short, which has—so I am told—increased the average length of life in these islands, by nearly one-third, since the first establishment of life insurances, one hundred and fifty years ago; every influence of this kind, I say, saves persons alive who would otherwise have died; and the great majority of these will be, even in surgical and zymotic cases, those of least resisting power, who are thus preserved to produce in time a still less powerful progeny.

Do I say that we ought not to save these people if we can? God forbid. The weakly, the diseased whether infant or adult, is here on earth; a British citizen; no more responsible for his own weakness than for his own existence. Society, that is, in plain English, we and our ancestors, are responsible for both; and we must fulfil the duty, and keep him in life; and, if we can, heal, strengthen, develop him to the utmost; and make the best of that which "fate and our own deservings" have given us to deal with. I do not speak of higher motives still; motives which, to every minister of religion, must be paramount and awful. I speak merely of physical and social motives, such as appeal to the conscience of every man—the instinct which bids every human-hearted man or woman to save life, alleviate pain, like Him who causes His sun to shine on the evil and on the good, and His rain to fall on the just and on the unjust.

But it is palpable that in doing so we must, year by year, preserve a large percentage of weakly persons who, marrying freely in their own class, must produce weaklier children, and they weaklier children still. Must, did I say? There are those who are of opinion—and I, after watching and comparing the histories of many families, indeed of every one with whom I have come in contact for now five-and-thirty years, in town and country, can only fear that their opinion is but too well founded on fact—that in the great majority of cases, in all classes whatsoever, the children are not equal to their parents, nor they, again, to their grand-parents of the beginning of the century; and that this degrading process goes on most surely and most rapidly in our large towns, and in proportion to the antiquity of those towns, and therefore in proportion to the number of generations during which the degrading influences have been at work.

This and cognate dangers have been felt more and more deeply, as the years have rolled on, by students of human society. To ward them off, theory after theory has been put on paper, especially in France, which deserve high praise for their ingenuity, less for their morality, and, I fear, still less for their common sense. For the theorist in his closet is certain to ignore, as inconvenient to the construction of his Utopia, certain of those broad facts of human nature which every active parish priest, medical man, or poor-law guardian has to face every day of his life.

Society and British human nature are what they have become by the indirect influences of long ages, and we can no more reconstruct the one than we can change the other. We can no more mend men by theories than we can by coercion—to which, by-the-bye, almost all these theorists look longingly as their final hope and mainstay. We must teach men to mend their own matters, of their own reason, and their own free-will. We must teach them that they are the arbiters of their own destinies; and, to a fearfully large degree, of their children's destinies after them. We must teach them not merely that they ought to be free, but that they are free, whether they know it or not, for good and for evil. And we must do that in this case, by teaching them sound practical science; the science of physiology as applied to health. So, and so only, can we cheek—I do not say stop entirely—though I believe even that to be ideally possible; but at least cheek the process of degradation which I believe to be surely going on, not merely in these islands, but in every civilised country in the world, in proportion to its civilisation.

It is still a question whether science has fully discovered those laws of hereditary health, the disregard of which causes so many marriages disastrous to generations yet unborn. But much valuable light has been thrown on this most mysterious and most important subject during the last few years. That light—and I thank God for it—is widening and deepening rapidly. And I doubt not that in a generation or two more, enough will be known to be thrown into the shape of practical and provable rules; and that, if not a public opinion, yet at least, what is more useful far, a wide-spread private opinion will grow up, especially among educated women, which will prevent many a tragedy and save many a life.

But, as to the laws of personal health: enough, and more than enough, is known already, to be applied

27

safely and easily by any adults, however unlearned, to the preservation not only of their own health, but of that of their children.

The value of healthy habitations, of personal cleanliness, of pure air and pure water, of various kinds of food, according as each tends to make bone, fat, or muscle, provided only—provided only—that the food be unadulterated; the value of various kinds of clothing, and physical exercise, of a free and equal development of the brain power, without undue overstrain in any one direction; in one word, the method of producing, as far as possible, the mentem sanam in corpore sano, and the wonderful and blessed effects of such obedience to those laws of nature, which are nothing but the good will of God expressed in facts—their wonderful and blessed tendency, I say, to eliminate the germs of hereditary disease, and to actually regenerate the human system—all this is known; known as fully and clearly as any human knowledge need be known; it is written in dozens of popular books and pamphlets. And why should this divine voice, which cries to man, tending to sink into effeminate barbarism through his own hasty and partial civilisation: "It is not too late. For your bodies, as for your spirits, there is an upward, as well as a downward path. You, or if not you, at least the children whom you have brought into the world, for whom you toil, for whom you hoard, for whom you pray, for whom you would give your lives,—they still may be healthy, strong, it may be beautiful, and have all the intellectual and social, as well as the physical advantages, which health, strength, and beauty give."—Ah, why is this divine voice now, as of old, Wisdom crying in the streets, and no man regarding her? I appeal to women, who are initiated, as we men can never be, into the stern mysteries of pain, and sorrow, and self-sacrifice;—they who bring forth children, weep over children, slave for children, and, if they have none of their own, then slave, with the holy instinct of the sexless bee, for the children of others—Let them say, shall this thing be?

Let my readers pardon me if I seem to write too earnestly. That I speak neither more nor less than the truth, every medical man knows full well. Not only as a very humble student of physiology, but as a parish priest of thirty years' standing, I have seen so much unnecessary misery; and I have in other cases seen similar misery so simply avoided; that the sense of the vastness of the evil is intensified by my sense of the easiness of the cure.

Why, then—to come to practical suggestions— should there not be opened in every great town in these realms a public school of health? It might connect itself with—I hold that it should form an integral part of—some existing educational institute. But it should at least give practical lectures, for fees small enough to put them within the reach of any respectable man or woman, however poor, I cannot but hope that such schools of health, if opened in the great manufacturing towns of England and Scotland, and, indeed, in such an Irish town as Belfast, would obtain pupils in plenty, and pupils who would thoroughly profit by what they hear. The people of these towns are, most of them, specially accustomed by their own trades to the application of scientific laws. To them, therefore, the application of any fresh physical laws to a fresh set of facts, would have nothing strange in it. They have already something of that inductive habit of mind which is the groundwork of all rational understanding or action. They would not turn the deaf and contemptuous ear with which the savage and the superstitious receive the revelation of nature's mysteries. Why should not, with so hopeful an audience, the experiment be tried far and wide, of giving lectures on health, as supplementary to those lectures on animal physiology which are, I am happy to say, becoming more and more common? Why should not people be taught— they are already being taught at Birmingham—something about the tissues of the body, their structure and uses, the circulation of the blood, respiration, chemical changes in the air respired, amount breathed, digestion, nature of food, absorption, secretion, structure of the nervous system—in fact, be taught something of how their own bodies are made and how they work? Teaching of this kind ought to, and will, in some more civilised age and country, be held a necessary element in the school course of every child, just as necessary as reading, writing, and arithmetic; for it is after all the most necessary branch of that "technical education" of which we hear so much just now, namely, the technic, or art, of keeping oneself alive and well.

But we can hardly stop there. After we have taught the condition of health, we must teach also the condition of disease; of those diseases specially which tend to lessen wholesale the health of townsfolk, exposed to an artificial mode of life. Surely young men and women should be taught something of the causes of zymotic disease, and of scrofula, consumption, rickets, dipsomania, cerebral derangement, and such like. They should be shown the practical value of pure air, pure water, unadulterated food, sweet and dry dwellings. Is there one of them, man or woman, who would not be the safer and happier, and the more useful to his or her neighbours, if they had acquired some sound notions about those questions of drainage on which their own lives and the lives of their children may every day depend? I say—women as well as men. I should have said women rather than men. For it is the women who have the ordering of the household, the bringing up of the children; the women who bide at home, while the men are away, it may be at the other end of the earth.

And if any say, as they have a right to say—"But these are subjects which can hardly be taught to young women in public lectures;" I rejoin—of course not, unless they are taught by women—by women, of course, duly educated and legally qualified. Let such teach to women, what every woman ought to know, and what her parents will very properly object to her hearing from almost any man. This is one of the main reasons why I have, for twenty years past, advocated the training of women for the medical profession; and one which countervails, in my mind, all possible objections to such a movement. And now, thank God, we are seeing the common sense of Great Britain, and indeed of every civilised nation, gradually coming round to that which seemed to me, when I first conceived of it, a dream too chimerical to be cherished save in secret—the restoring woman to her natural share in that sacred office of healer, which she held in the Middle Ages, and from which she was thrust out during the sixteenth century.

I am most happy to see, for instance, that the National Health Society,[3] which I earnestly recommend to the attention of my readers, announces a "Course of Lectures for Ladies on Elementary Physiology and Hygiene," by a lady, to which I am also most happy to see, governesses are admitted at half-fees. Alas! how much misery, disease, and even death might have been prevented, had governesses been taught such matters thirty years ago, I, for one, know too well. May the day soon come when there will be educated women enough to give such lectures throughout these realms, to rich as well as poor—for the rich, strange to say, need them often as much as the poor do—and that we may live to see, in every great town, health classes for women as well as for men, sending forth year by year more young women and young men taught, not only to take care of themselves and of their families, but to exercise moral influence over their fellow-citizens, as

---

3   9, Adam Street, Adelphi, London.

champions in the battle against dirt and drunkenness, disease and death.

There may be those who would answer—or rather, there would certainly have been those who would have so answered thirty years ago, before the so-called materialism of advanced science had taught us some practical wisdom about education, and reminded people that they have bodies as well as minds and souls—"You say, we are likely to grow weaklier, unhealthier. And if it were so, what matter? Mind makes the man, not body. We do not want our children to be stupid giants and bravos; but clever, able, highly educated, however weakly Providence or the laws of nature may have chosen to make them. Let them overstrain their brains a little; let them contract their chests, and injure their digestion and their eyesight, by sitting at desks, poring over books. Intellect is what we want. Intellect makes money. Intellect makes the world. We would rather see our son a genius than a mere athlete." Well: and so would I. But what if intellect alone does not even make money, save as Messrs. Dodson and Fogg, Sampson Brass, and Montagu Tigg were wont to make it, unless backed by an able, enduring, healthy physique, such as I have seen, almost without exception, in those successful men of business whom I have had the honour and the pleasure of knowing? What if intellect, or what is now called intellect, did not make the world, or the smallest wheel or cog of it? What if, for want of obeying the laws of nature, parents bred up neither a genius nor an athlete, but only an incapable unhappy personage, with a huge upright forehead, like that of a Byzantine Greek, filled with some sort of pap instead of brains, and tempted alternately to fanaticism and strong drink? We must, in the great majority of cases, have the *corpus sanem* if we want the *mentem sanem;* and healthy bodies are the only trustworthy organs for healthy minds. Which is cause and which is effect, I shall not stay to debate here. But wherever we find a population generally weakly, stunted, scrofulous, we find in them a corresponding type of brain, which cannot be trusted to do good work; which is capable more or less of madness, whether solitary or epidemic. It may be very active; it may be very quick at catching at new and grand ideas—all the more quick, perhaps, on account of its own secret malaise and self-discontent; but it will be irritable, spasmodic, hysterical. It will be apt to mistake capacity of talk for capacity of action, excitement for earnestness, virulence for force, and, too often; cruelty for justice. It will lose manful independence, individuality, originality; and when men act, they will act from the consciousness of personal weakness, like sheep rushing over a hedge, leaning against each other, exhorting each other to be brave, and swaying about in mobs and masses. These were the intellectual weaknesses which, as I read history, followed on physical degradation in Imperial Rome, in Alexandria, in Byzantium. Have we not seen them reappear, under fearful forms, in Paris but the other day?

I do not blame; I do not judge. My theory, which I hold, and shall hold, to be fairly founded on a wide induction, forbids me to blame and to judge; because it tells me that these defects are mainly physical; that those who exhibit them are mainly to be pitied, as victims of the sins or ignorance of their forefathers.

But it tells me too, that those who, professing to be educated men, and therefore bound to know better, treat these physical phenomena as spiritual, healthy, and praiseworthy; who even exasperate them, that they may make capital out of the weaknesses of fallen man, are the most contemptible and yet the most dangerous of public enemies, let them cloak their quackery under whatsoever patriotic, or scientific, or even sacred words.

There are those again honest, kindly, sensible, practical men, many of them; men whom I have no wish to offend; whom I had rather ask to teach me some of their own experience and common sense, which has learned to discern, like good statesmen, not only what ought to be done, but what can be done—there are those, I say, who would sooner see this whole question let alone. Their feeling, as far as I can analyse it, seems to be that the evils of which I have been complaining, are on the whole inevitable; or, if not, that we can mend so very little of them, that it is wisest to leave them alone altogether, lest, like certain sewers, "the more you stir them, the more they smell." They fear lest we should unsettle the minds of the many for whom these evils will never be mended; lest we make them discontented; discontented with their houses, their occupations, their food, their whole social arrangements; and all in vain.

I should answer, in all courtesy and humility—for I sympathise deeply with such men and women, and respect them deeply likewise—but are not people discontented already, from the lowest to the highest? And ought a man, in such a piecemeal, foolish, greedy, sinful world as this is, and always has been, to be anything but discontented? If he thinks that things are going all right, must he not have a most beggarly conception of what going right means? And if things are not going right, can it be anything but good for him to see that they are not going right? Can truth and fact harm any human being? I shall not believe so, as long as I have a Bible wherein to believe. For my part, I should like to make every man, woman, and child whom I meet discontented with themselves, even as I am discontented with myself. I should like to awaken in them, about their physical, their intellectual, their moral condition, that divine discontent which is the parent, first of upward aspiration and then of self-control, thought, effort to fulfil that aspiration even in part. For to be discontented with the divine discontent, and to be ashamed with the noble shame, is the very germ and first upgrowth of all virtue. Men begin at first, as boys begin when they grumble at their school and their schoolmasters, to lay the blame on others; to be discontented with their circumstances—the things which stand around them; and to cry, "Oh that I had this!" "Oh that I had that!" But by that way no deliverance lies. That discontent only ends in revolt and rebellion, social or political; and that, again, still in the same worship of circumstances—but this time desperate—which ends, let it disguise itself under what fine names it will, in what the old Greeks called a tyranny; in which—as in the Spanish republics of America, and in France more than once—all have become the voluntary slaves of one man, because each man fancies that the one man can improve his circumstances for him.

But the wise man will learn, like Epictetus the heroic slave, the slave of Epaphroditus, Nero's minion—and in what baser and uglier circumstances could human being find himself?—to find out the secret of being truly free; namely, to be discontented with no man and no thing save himself. To say not—"Oh that I had this and that!" but "Oh that I were this and that!" Then, by God's help—and that heroic slave, heathen though he was, believed and trusted in God's help—"I will make myself that which God has shown me that I ought to be and can be."

Ten thousand a year, or ten million a year, as Epictetus saw full well, cannot mend that vulgar discontent with circumstances which he had felt—and who with more right?—and conquered, and despised. For that is the discontent of children, wanting always more holidays and more sweets. But I wish my readers to have, and to cherish, the discontent of men and women.

Therefore I would make men and women discontented, with the divine and wholesome discontent, at their own physical frame, and at that of their children. I would accustom their eyes to those precious heirlooms of the human race, the statues of the old Greeks; to their tender grandeur, their chaste healthfulness, their unconscious, because perfect might: and say—There; these are tokens to you, and to all generations yet unborn, of what man could be once; of what he can be again if he will obey those laws of nature which are the voice of God. I would make them discontented with the ugliness and closeness of their dwellings; I would make them discontented with the fashion of their garments, and still more just now the women, of all ranks, with the fashion of theirs; and with everything around them which they have the power of improving, if it be at all ungraceful, superfluous, tawdry, ridiculous, unwholesome. I would make them discontented with what they call their education, and say to them—You call the three Royal R's education? They are not education: no more is the knowledge which would enable you to take the highest prizes given by the Society of Arts, or any other body. They are not education: they are only instruction; a necessary groundwork, in an age like this, for making practical use of your education: but not the education itself.

And if they asked me, What then education meant? I should point them, first, I think, to noble old Lilly's noble old "Euphues," of three hundred years ago, and ask them to consider what it says about education, and especially this passage concerning that mere knowledge which is nowadays strangely miscalled education. "There are two principal and peculiar gifts in the nature of man, knowledge and reason. The one"—that is reason—"commandeth, and the other"—that is knowledge—"obeyeth. These things neither the whirling wheel of fortune can change, nor the deceitful cavillings of worldlings separate, neither sickness abate, nor age abolish." And next I should point them to those pages in Mr. Gladstone's "Juventus Mundi," where he describes the ideal training of a Greek youth in Homer's days; and say—There: that is an education fit for a really civilised man, even though he never saw a book in his life; the full, proportionate, harmonious educing-that is, bringing out and developing—of all the faculties of his body, mind, and heart, till he becomes at once a reverent yet self-assured, a graceful and yet a valiant, an able and yet an eloquent personage.

And if any should say to me—"But what has this to do with science? Homer's Greeks knew no science;" I should rejoin—But they had, pre-eminently above all ancient races which we know, the scientific instinct; the teachableness and modesty; the clear eye and quick ear; the hearty reverence for fact and nature, and for the human body, and mind, and spirit; for human nature in a word, in its completeness, as the highest fact upon this earth. Therefore they became in after years, not only the great colonisers and the great civilisers of the old world—the most practical people, I hold, which the world ever saw; but the parents of all sound physics as well as of all sound metaphysics. Their very religion, in spite of its imperfections, helped forward their education, not in spite of, but by means of that anthropomorphism which we sometimes too hastily decry. As Mr. Gladstone says: "As regarded all other functions of our nature, outside the domain of the life to Godward—all those functions which are summed up in what St. Paul calls the flesh and the mind, the psychic and bodily life, the tendency of the system was to exalt the human element, by proposing a model of beauty, strength, and wisdom, in all their combinations, so elevated that the effort to attain them required a continual upward strain. It made divinity attainable; and thus it effectually directed the thought and aim of man

Along the line of limitless desires.

Such a scheme of religion, though failing grossly in the government of the passions, and in upholding the standard of moral duties, tended powerfully to produce a lofty self-respect, and a large, free, and varied conception of humanity. It incorporated itself in schemes of notable discipline for mind and body, indeed of a lifelong education; and these habits of mind and action had their marked results (to omit many other greatnesses) in a philosophy, literature, and art, which remain to this day unrivalled or unsurpassed."

So much those old Greeks did for their own education, without science and without Christianity. We who have both: what might we not do, if we would be true to our advantages, and to ourselves?

THE TWO BREATHS [4]

Ladies,—I have been honoured by a second invitation to address you, and I dare not refuse it; because it gives me an opportunity of speaking on a matter, knowledge and ignorance about which may seriously affect your health and happiness, and that of the children with whom you may have to do. I must apologise if I say many things which are well known to many persons in this room: they ought to be well known to all: but it is generally best to assume total ignorance in one's hearers, and to begin from the beginning.

I shall try to be as simple as possible; to trouble you as little as possible with scientific terms; to be practical; and at the same time, if possible, interesting.

I should wish to call this lecture "The Two Breaths:" not merely "The Breath;" and for this reason: every time you breathe you breathe two different breaths; you take in one, you give out another. The composition of those two breaths is different. Their effects are different. The breath which has been breathed out must not be breathed in again. To tell you why it

---

4   A Lecture delivered at Winchester, May 31, 1869.

must not would lead me into anatomical details, not quite in place here as yet; though the day will come, I trust, when every woman entrusted with the care of children will be expected to know something about them. But this I may say: Those who habitually take in fresh breath will probably grow up large, strong, ruddy, cheerful, active, clear-headed, fit for their work. Those who habitually take in the breath which has been breathed out by themselves, or any other living creature, will certainly grow up, if they grow up at all, small, weak, pale, nervous, depressed, unfit for work, and tempted continually to resort to stimulants, and become drunkards.

If you want to see how different the breath breathed out is from the breath taken in, you have only to try a somewhat cruel experiment, but one which people too often try upon themselves, their children, and their workpeople. If you take any small animal with lungs like your own—a mouse, for instance—and force it to breathe no air but what you have breathed already; if you put it in a close box, and while you take in breath from the outer air, send out your breath through a tube, into that box, the animal will soon faint: if you go on long with this process, it will die.

Take a second instance, which I beg to press most seriously on the notice of mothers, governesses, and nurses. If you allow a child to get into the habit of sleeping with its head under the bed-clothes, and thereby breathing its own breath over and over again, that child will assuredly grow pale, weak, and ill.

Medical men have cases on record of scrofula appearing in children previously healthy, which could only be accounted for from this habit, and which ceased when the habit stopped. Let me again entreat your attention to this undoubted fact.

Take another instance, which is only too common: If you are in a crowded room, with plenty of fire and lights and company, doors and windows all shut tight, how often you feel faint—so faint that you may require smelling-salts or some other stimulant. The cause of your faintness is just the same as that of the mouse's fainting in the box; you and your friends, and, as I shall show you presently, the fire and the candles likewise, having been all breathing each other's breaths, over and over again, till the air has become unfit to support life. You are doing your best to enact over again the Highland tragedy, of which Sir James Simpson tells in his lectures to the working-classes of Edinburgh, when at a Christmas meeting thirty-six persons danced all night in a small room with a low ceiling, keeping the doors and windows shut. The atmosphere of the room was noxious beyond description; and the effect was, that seven of the party were soon after seized with typhus fever, of which two died. You are inflicting on yourselves the torments of the poor dog, who is kept at the Grotto del Cane, near Naples, to be stupefied, for the amusement of visitors, by the carbonic acid gas of the Grotto, and brought to life again by being dragged into the fresh air; nay, you are inflicting upon yourselves the torments of the famous

Black Hole of Calcutta: and, if there was no chimney in the room, by which some fresh air could enter, the candles would soon burn blue, as they do, you know, when ghosts appear; your brains become disturbed; and you yourselves ran the risk of becoming ghosts, and the candles of actually going out.

Of this last fact there is no doubt; for if, instead of putting a mouse into the box, you will put a lighted candle, and breathe into the tube as before, however gently, you will in a short time put the candle out.

Now, how is this? First, what is the difference between the breath you take in and the breath you give out? And next, why has it a similar effect on animal life and a lighted candle?

The difference is this. The breath which you take in is, or ought to be, pure air, composed, on the whole, of oxygen and nitrogen, with a minute portion of carbonic acid.

The breath which you give out is an impure air, to which has been added, among other matters which will not support life, an excess of carbonic acid.

That this is the fact you can prove for yourselves by a simple experiment. Get a little lime-water at the chemist's, and breathe into it through a glass tube; your breath will at once make the lime-water milky. The carbonic acid of your breath has laid hold of the lime, and made it visible as white carbonate of lime—in plain English, as common chalk.

Now I do not wish, as I said, to load your memories with scientific terms: but I beseech you to remember

44

at least these two, oxygen gas and carbonic acid gas; and to remember that, as surely as oxygen feeds the fire of life, so surely does carbonic acid put it out.

I say, "the fire of life." In that expression lies the answer to our second question: Why does our breath produce a similar effect upon the mouse and the lighted candle? Every one of us is, as it were, a living fire. Were we not, how could we be always warmer than the air outside us? There is a process; going on perpetually in each of us, similar to that by which coals are burnt in the fire, oil in a lamp, wax in a candle, and the earth itself in a volcano. To keep each of those fires alight, oxygen is needed; and the products of combustion, as they are called, are more or less the same in each case—carbonic acid and steam.

These facts justify the expression I just made use of—which may have seemed to some of you fantastical—that the fire and the candles in the crowded room were breathing the same breath as you were. It is but too true. An average fire in the grate requires, to keep it burning, as much oxygen as several human beings do; each candle or lamp must have its share of oxygen likewise, and that a very considerable one, and an average gas-burner—pray attend to this, you who live in rooms lighted with gas—consumes as much oxygen as several candles. All alike are making carbonic acid. The carbonic acid of the fire happily escapes up the chimney in the smoke: but the carbonic acid from the human beings and the candles remains to poison the room, unless it be ventilated.

45

Now, I think you may understand one of the simplest, and yet most terrible, cases of want of ventilation—death by the fumes of charcoal. A human being shut up in a room, of which every crack is closed, with a pan of burning charcoal, falls asleep, never to wake again. His inward fire is competing with the fire of charcoal for the oxygen of the room; both are making carbonic acid out of it: but the charcoal, being the stronger of the two, gets all the oxygen to itself, and leaves the human being nothing to inhale but the carbonic acid which it has made. The human being, being the weaker, dies first: but the charcoal dies also. When it has exhausted all the oxygen of the room, it cools, goes out, and is found in the morning half-consumed beside its victim. If you put a giant or an elephant, I should conceive, into that room, instead of a human being, the case would be reversed for a time: the elephant would put out the burning charcoal by the carbonic acid from his mighty lungs; and then, when he had exhausted all the air in the room, die likewise of his own carbonic acid.

Now, I think, we may see what ventilation means, and why it is needed.

Ventilation means simply letting out the foul air, and letting in the fresh air; letting out the air which has been breathed by men or by candles, and letting in the air which has not. To understand how to do that, we must remember a most simple chemical law, that a gas as it is warmed expands, and therefore becomes lighter; as it cools, it contracts, and becomes heavier.

46

Now the carbonic acid in the breath which comes out of our mouth is warm, lighter than the air, and rises to the ceiling; and therefore in any unventilated room full of people, there is a layer of foul air along the ceiling. You might soon test that for yourselves, if you could mount a ladder and put your heads there aloft. You do test it for yourselves when you sit in the galleries of churches and theatres, where the air is palpably more foul, and therefore more injurious, than down below.

Where, again, work-people are employed in a crowded house of many storeys, the health of those who work on the upper floors always suffers most.

In the old monkey-house of the Zoological Gardens, when the cages were on the old plan, tier upon tier, the poor little fellows in the uppermost tier—so I have been told—always died first of the monkey's constitutional complaint, consumption, simply from breathing the warm breath of their friends below. But since the cages have been altered, and made to range side by side from top to bottom, consumption—I understand—has vastly diminished among them.

The first question in ventilation, therefore, is to get this carbonic acid safe out of the room, while it is warm and light and close to the ceiling; for if you do not, this happens: The carbonic acid gas cools and becomes heavier; for carbonic acid, at the same temperature as common air, is so much heavier than common air, that you may actually—if you are handy enough—turn it from one vessel to another, and pour out for your enemy a glass of invisible poison. So down to the floor this heavy carbonic acid comes, and lies along it, just as it lies often in the bottom of old wells, or old brewers' vats, as a stratum of poison, killing occasionally the men who descend into it. Hence, as foolish a practice as I know is that of sleeping on the floor; for towards the small hours, when the room gets cold, the sleeper on the floor is breathing carbonic acid.

And here one word to those ladies who interest themselves with the poor. The poor are too apt in times of distress to pawn their bedsteads and keep their beds. Never, if you have influence, let that happen. Keep the bedstead, whatever else may go, to save the sleeper from the carbonic acid on the floor.

How, then, shall we get rid of the foul air at the top of the room? After all that has been written and tried on ventilation, I know no simpler method than putting into the chimney one of Arnott's ventilators, which may be bought and fixed for a few shillings; always remembering that it must be. fixed into the chimney as near the ceiling as possible. I can speak of these ventilators from twenty-five years' experience. Living in a house with low ceilings, liable to become overcharged with carbonic acid, which produces sleepiness in the evening, I have found that these ventilators keep the air fresh and pure; and I consider the presence of one of these ventilators in a room more valuable than three or four feet additional height of ceiling. I have found, too, that their working proves how necessary they are, from this simple fact:

You would suppose that, as the ventilator opens freely into the chimney, the smoke would be blown down through it in high winds, and blacken the ceiling: but this is just what does not happen. If the ventilator be at all properly poised, so as to shut with a violent gust of wind, it will at all other moments keep itself permanently open; proving thereby that there is an up-draught of heated air continually escaping from the ceiling up the chimney. Another very simple method of ventilation is employed in those excellent cottages which Her Majesty has built for her labourers round Windsor. Over each door a sheet of perforated zinc, some eighteen inches square, is fixed; allowing the foul air to escape into the passage; and in the ceiling of the passage a similar sheet of zinc, allowing it to escape into the roof. Fresh air, meanwhile, should be obtained from outside, by piercing the windows, or otherwise. And here let me give one hint to all builders of houses: If possible, let bedroom windows open at the top as well as at the bottom.

Let me impress the necessity of using some such contrivances, not only on parents and educators, but on those who employ workpeople, and above all on those who employ young women in shops or in workrooms. What their condition may be in this city I know not; but most painful it has been to me in other places, when passing through warehouses or workrooms, to see the pale, sodden, and, as the French would say, "etiolated" countenances of the girls who were passing the greater part of the day in them; and painful, also, to breathe an atmosphere of which habit had, alas! made them unconscious, but which to one coming out of the open air was altogether noxious, and shocking also; for it was fostering the seeds of death, not only in the present but future generations.

Why should this be? Everyone will agree that good ventilation is necessary in a hospital, because people cannot get well without fresh air. Do they not see that by the same reasoning good ventilation is necessary everywhere, because people cannot remain well without fresh air? Let me entreat those who employ women in workrooms, if they have no time to read through such books as Dr. Andrew Combe's "Physiology applied to Health and Education," and Madame de Wahl's "Practical Hints on the Moral, Mental, and Physical Training of Girls," to procure certain tracts published by Messrs. Jarrold, Paternoster Row, for the Ladies' Sanitary Association; especially one which bears on this subject: "The Black-hole in our own Bedrooms;" Dr. Lankester's "School Manual of Health;" or a manual on ventilation, published by the Metropolitan Working Classes Association for the Improvement of Public Health.

I look forward—I say it openly—to some period of higher civilisation, when the Acts of Parliament for the ventilation of factories and workshops shall be largely extended, and made far more stringent; when officers of public health shall be empowered to enforce the ventilation of every room in which persons are employed for hire: and empowered also to demand a proper system of ventilation for every new house, whether in country or in town. To that, I believe, we must come: but I had sooner far see these improvements carried out, as befits the citizens of a free country, in the spirit of the Gospel rather than in that of the Law; carried out, not compulsorily and from fear of fines, but voluntarily, from a sense of duty, honour, and humanity. I appeal, therefore, to the good feeling of all whom it may concern, whether the health of those whom they employ, and therefore the supply of fresh air which they absolutely need, are not matters for which they are not, more or less, responsible to their country and their God.

And if any excellent person of the old school should answer me: "Why make all this fuss about ventilation? Our forefathers got on very well without it"—I must answer that, begging their pardons, our ancestors did nothing of the kind. Our ancestors got on usually very ill in these matters: and when they got on well, it was because they had good ventilation in spite of themselves.

First. They got on very ill. To quote a few remarkable instances of longevity, or to tell me that men were larger and stronger on the average in old times, is to yield to the old fallacy of fancying that savages were peculiarly healthy, because those who were seen were active and strong. The simple answer is, that the strong alone survived, while the majority died from the severity of the training. Savages do not increase in number; and our ancestors increased but very slowly for many centuries. I am not going to disgust my audience with statistics of disease: but knowing something, as I happen to do, of the social state and of the health of the Middle and Elizabethan Ages, I have no hesitation in saying that the average of disease and death was far greater then than it is now. Epidemics of many kinds, typhus, ague, plague—all diseases which were caused more or less by bad air—devastated this land and Europe in those days with a horrible intensity, to which even the choleras of our times are mild. The back streets, the hospitals, the gaols, the barracks, the camps—every place in which any large number of persons congregated, were so many nests of pestilence, engendered by uncleanliness, which defiled alike the water which was drunk and the air which was breathed; and as a single fact, of which the tables of insurance companies assure us, the average of human life in England has increased twenty-five per cent. since the reign of George I., owing simply to our more rational and cleanly habits of life.

But secondly, I said that when our ancestors got on well, they did so because they got ventilation in spite of themselves. Luckily for them, their houses were ill-built; their doors and windows would not shut. They had lattice-windowed houses, too; to live in one of which, as I can testify from long experience, is as thoroughly ventilating as living in a lantern with the horn broken out. It was because their houses were full of draughts, and still more, in the early Middle Age, because they had no glass, and stopped out the air only by a shutter at night, that they sought for shelter rather than for fresh air, of which they sometimes had too much; and, to escape the wind, built their houses in holes, such as that in which the old city of Winchester stands. Shelter, I believe, as much as the desire to be near fish in Lent, and to occupy the rich alluvium of the valleys, made the monks of Old England choose the river-banks for the sites of their abbeys. They made a mistake therein, which, like most mistakes, did not go unpunished. These low situations, especially while the forests were yet thick on the hills around, were the perennial haunts of fever and ague, produced by subtle vegetable poisons, carried in the carbonic acid given off by rotten vegetation. So there, again, they fell in with man's old enemy—bad air. Still, as long as the doors and windows did not shut, some free circulation of air remained. But now, our doors and windows shut only too tight. We have plate-glass instead of lattices; and we have replaced the draughty and smoky, but really wholesome open chimney, with its wide corners and settles, by narrow registers, and even by stoves. We have done all we can, in fact, to seal ourselves up hermetically from the outer air, and to breath our own breaths over and over again; and we pay the penalty of it in a thousand ways unknown to our ancestors, through whose rooms all the winds of heaven whistled, and who were glad enough to shelter themselves from draughts in the sitting-room by the high screen round the fire, and in the sleeping-room by the thick curtains of the four-post bedstead, which is now rapidly disappearing before a higher civilisation. We therefore absolutely require to make for ourselves the very ventilation from which our ancestors tried to escape.

But, ladies, there is an old and true proverb, that you may bring a horse to the water, but you cannot make him drink. And in like wise it is too true, that you may bring people to the fresh air, but you cannot make them breath it. Their own folly, or the folly of their parents and educators, prevents their lungs being duly filled and duly emptied. Therefore the blood is not duly oxygenated, and the whole system goes wrong. Paleness, weakness, consumption, scrofula, and too many other ailments, are the consequences of ill-filled lungs. For without well-filled lungs, robust health is impossible.

And if anyone shall answer: "We do not want robust health so much as intellectual attainment; the mortal body, being the lower organ, must take its chance, and be even sacrificed, if need be to the higher organ—the immortal mind"—To such I reply, You cannot do it. The laws of nature, which are the express will of God, laugh such attempts to scorn. Every organ of the body is formed out of the blood; and if the blood be vitiated, every organ suffers in proportion to its delicacy; and the brain, being the most delicate and highly specialised of all organs, suffers most of all, and soonest of all, as everyone knows who has tried to work his brain when his digestion was the least out of order. Nay, the very

morals will suffer. From ill-filled lungs, which sig-
nify ill-repaired blood, arise year by year an amount
not merely of disease, but of folly, temper, laziness,
intemperance, madness, and, let me tell you fairly,
crime—the sum of which will never be known till that
great day when men shall be called to account for all
deeds done in the body, whether they be good or evil.

I must refer you on this subject again to Andrew
Combe's "Physiology," especially chapters iv. and vii.;
and also to chapter x. of Madame de Wahl's excellent
book. I will only say this shortly, that the three most
common causes of ill-filled lungs, in children and in
young ladies, are stillness, silence, and stays.

First, stillness; a sedentary life, and want of exercise. A girl is kept for hours sitting on a form writing
or reading, to do which she must lean forward; and
if her schoolmistress cruelly attempts to make her sit
upright, and thereby keep the spine in an attitude for
which Nature did not intend it, she is thereby doing
her best to bring on that disease, so fearfully common in girls' schools, lateral curvature of the spine.
But practically the girl will stoop forward. And what
happens? The lower ribs are pressed into the body,
thereby displacing more or less something inside. The
diaphragm in the meantime, which is the very bel-
lows of the lungs, remains loose; the lungs are never
properly filled or emptied; and an excess of carbonic
acid accumulates at the bottom of them. What follows? Frequent sighing to get rid of it; heaviness of
head; depression of the whole nervous system under

the influence of the poison of the lungs; and when the poor child gets up from her weary work, what is the first thing she probably does? She lifts up her chest, stretches, yawns, and breathes deeply—Nature's voice, Nature's instinctive cure, which is probably regarded as ungraceful, as what is called "lolling" is. As if sitting upright was not an attitude in itself essentially ungraceful, and such as no artist would care to draw. As if "lolling," which means putting the body in the attitude of the most perfect ease compatible with a fully-expanded chest, was not in itself essentially graceful, and to be seen in every reposing figure in Greek bas-reliefs and vases; graceful, and like all graceful actions, healthful at the same time. The only tolerably wholesome attitude of repose, which I see allowed in average school-rooms, is lying on the back on the floor, or on a sloping board, in which case the lungs must be fully expanded. But even so, a pillow, or some equivalent, ought to be placed under the small of the back: or the spine will be strained at its very weakest point.

I now go on to the second mistake—enforced silence. Moderate reading aloud is good: but where there is any tendency to irritability of throat or lungs, too much moderation cannot be used. You may as well try to cure a diseased lung by working it, as to cure a lame horse by galloping him. But where the breathing organs are of average health let it be said once and for all, that children and young people cannot make too much noise. The parents who cannot bear the noise of their children have no right to have brought them into the world. The schoolmistress who enforces silence on her pupils is committing—unintentionally no doubt, but still committing—an offence against reason, worthy only of a convent. Every shout, every burst of laughter, every song—nay, in the case of infants, as physiologists well know, every moderate fit of crying—conduces to health, by rapidly filling and emptying the lung, and changing the blood more rapidly from black to red, that is, from death to life. Andrew Combe tells a story of a large charity school, in which the young girls were, for the sake of their health, shut up in the hall and school-room during play hours, from November till March, and no romping or noise allowed. The natural consequences were, the great majority of them fell ill; and I am afraid that a great deal of illness has been from time to time contracted in certain school-rooms, simply through this one cause of enforced silence. Some cause or other there must be for the amount of ill-health and weakliness which prevails especially among girls of the middle classes in towns, who have not, poor things, the opportunities which richer girls have, of keeping themselves in strong health by riding, skating, archery,—that last quite an admirable exercise for the chest and lungs, and far preferable to croquet, which involves too much unwholesome stooping.—Even a game of ball, if milliners and shop-girls had room to indulge in one after their sedentary work, might bring fresh spirits to many a heart, and fresh colour to many a cheek.

I spoke just now of the Greeks. I suppose you will all allow that the Greeks were, as far as we know, the most beautiful race which the world ever saw. Every educated man knows that they were also the cleverest of all races; and, next to his Bible, thanks, God for Greek literature.

Now, these people had made physical as well as intellectual education a science as well as a study. Their women practised graceful, and in some cases even athletic, exercises. They developed, by a free and healthy life, those figures which remain everlasting and unapproachable models of human beauty: but—to come to my third point—they wore no stays. The first mention of stays that I have ever found is in the letters of dear old Synesius, Bishop of Cyrene, on the Greek coast of Africa, about four hundred years after the Christian era. He tells us how, when he was shipwrecked on a remote part of the coast, and he and the rest of the passengers were starving on cockles and limpets, there was among them a slave girl out of the far East, who had a pinched wasp-waist, such as you may see on the old Hindoo sculptures, and such as you may see in any street in a British town. And when the Greek ladies of the neighbourhood found her out, they sent for her from house to house, to behold, with astonishment and laughter, this new and prodigious, waist, with which it seemed to them it was impossible for a human being to breathe or live; and they petted the poor girl, and fed her, as they might a dwarf or a giantess, till she got quite fat and comfortable, while her owners had not enough to eat. So strange and ridiculous seemed our present fashion to the descendants of those who, centuries before, had imagined, because they had seen living and moving, those glorious statues which we pretend to admire, but refuse to imitate.

It seems to me that a few centuries hence, when mankind has learnt to fear God more, and therefore to obey more strictly those laws of nature and of science which are the will of God—it seems to me, I say, that in those days the present fashion of tight lacing will be looked back upon as a contemptible and barbarous superstition, denoting a very low level of civilisation in the peoples which have practised it. That for generations past women should have been in the habit—not to please men, who do not care about the matter as a point of beauty—but simply to vie with each other in obedience to something called fashion—that they should, I say, have been in the habit of deliberately crushing that part of the body which should be specially left free, contracting and displacing their lungs, their heart, and all the most vital and important organs, and entailing thereby disease, not only on themselves but on their children after them; that for forty years past physicians should have been telling them of the folly of what they have been doing; and that they should as yet, in the great majority of cases, not only turn a deaf ear to all warnings, but actually deny the offence, of which one glance of the physician or the sculptor, who know what shape the human body ought to be, brings them in guilty—this,

I say, is an instance of—what shall I call it?—which deserves at once the lash, not merely of the satirist, but of any theologian who really believes that God made the physical universe. Let me, I pray you, appeal to your common sense for a moment. When any one chooses a horse or a dog, whether for strength, for speed, or for any other useful purpose, the first thing almost to be looked at is the girth round the ribs; the room for heart and lungs. Exactly in proportion to that will be the animal's general healthiness, power of endurance, and value in many other ways. If you will look at eminent lawyers and famous orators, who have attained a healthy old age, you will see that in every case they are men, like the late Lord Palmerston, and others whom I could mention, of remarkable size, not merely in the upper, but in the lower part of the chest; men who had, therefore, a peculiar power of using the diaphragm to fill and to clear the lungs, and therefore to oxygenate the blood of the whole body. Now, it is just these lower ribs, across which the diaphragm is stretched like the head of a drum, which stays contract to a minimum. If you advised owners of horses and hounds to put their horses or their hounds into stays, and lace them up tight, in order to increase their beauty, you would receive, I doubt not, a very courteous, but certainly a very decided, refusal to do that which would spoil not merely the animals themselves, but the whole stud or the whole kennel for years to come. And if you advised an orator to put himself into tight stays, he, no doubt, again would give a courteous

answer; but he would reply—if he was a really educated man—that to comply with your request would
involve his giving up public work, under the probable
penalty of being dead within the twelve-month.

And how much work of every kind, intellectual
as well as physical, is spoiled or hindered; how many
deaths occur from consumption and other complaints
which are the result of this habit of tight lacing, is
known partly to the medical men, who lift up their
voices in vain, and known fully to Him who will not
interfere with the least of His own physical laws to
save human beings from the consequences of their
own wilful folly.

And now—to end this lecture with more pleas-
ing thoughts—What becomes of this breath which
passes from your lips? Is it merely harmful; merely
waste? God forbid! God has forbidden that anything
should be merely harmful or merely waste in this so
wise and well-made world. The carbonic acid which
passes from your lips at every breath—ay, even that
which oozes from the volcano crater when the erup-
tion is past—is a precious boon to thousands of
things of which you have daily need. Indeed there is
a sort of hint at physical truth in the old fairy tale of
the girl, from whose lips, as she spoke, fell pearls and
diamonds; for the carbonic acid of your breath may
help hereafter to make the pure carbonate of lime
of a pearl, or the still purer carbon of a diamond.
Nay, it may go—in such a world of transformations
do we live—to make atoms of coal strata, which

after being buried for ages beneath deep seas, shall be upheaved in continents which are yet unborn, and there be burnt for the use of a future race of men, and resolved into their original elements. Coal, wise men tell us, is on the whole breath and sunlight; the breath of living creatures who have lived in the vast swamps and forests of some primeval world, and the sunlight which transmuted that breath into the leaves and stems of trees, magically locked up for ages in that black stone, to become, when it is burnt at last, light and carbonic acid as it was at first. For though you must not breathe your breath again, you may at least eat your breath, if you will allow the sun to transmute it for you into vegetables; or you may enjoy its fragrance and its colour in the shape of a lily or a rose. When you walk in a sunlit garden, every word you speak, every breath you breathe, is feeding the plants and flowers around. The delicate surface of the green leaves absorbs the carbonic acid, and parts it into its elements, retaining the carbon to make woody fibre, and courteously returning you the oxygen to mingle with the fresh air, and be inhaled by your lungs once more. Thus do you feed the plants; just as the plants feed you: while the great life-giving sun feeds both; and the geranium standing in the sick child's window does not merely rejoice his eye and mind by its beauty and freshness, but repays honestly the trouble spent on it; absorbing the breath which the child needs not, and giving to him the breath which he needs.

So are the services of all things constituted according to a Divine and wonderful order, and knit together in mutual dependence and mutual helpfulness—a fact to be remembered with hope and comfort: but also with awe and fear. For as in that which is above nature, so in nature itself; he that breaks one physical law is guilty of all. The whole universe, as it were, takes up arms against him; and all nature, with her numberless and unseen powers, is ready to avenge herself on him, and on his children after him, he knows not when nor where. He, on the other hand, who obeys the laws of nature with his whole heart and mind, will find all things working together to him for good. He is at peace with the physical universe. He is helped and befriended alike by the sun above his head and the dust beneath his feet; because he is obeying the will and mind of Him who made sun, and dust, and all things; and who has given them a law which cannot be broken.

THRIFT [5]

Ladies,—I have chosen for the title of this lecture a practical and prosaic word, because I intend the lecture itself to be as practical and prosaic as I can make it, without becoming altogether dull.

The question of the better or worse education of women is one far too important for vague sentiment, wild aspirations, or Utopian dreams.

It is a practical question, on which depends not merely money or comfort, but too often health and life, as the consequences of a good education, or disease and death—I know too well of what I speak—as the consequences of a bad one.

I beg you, therefore, to put out of your minds at the outset any fancy that I wish for a social revolution in the position of women; or that I wish to see them educated by exactly the same methods, and in exactly the same subjects, as men. British lads, on an average, are far too ill-taught still, in spite of all recent improvements, for me to wish that British girls should be taught in the same way.

---

5   Lecture delivered at Winchester, March 17, 1869.

Moreover, whatever defects there may have been—and defects there must be in all things human—in the past education of British women, it has been most certainly a splendid moral success. It has made, by the grace of God, British women the best wives, mothers, daughters, sisters, aunts, that the world, as far as I can discover, has yet seen.

Let those who will, sneer at the women of England. We who have to do the work and to fight the battle of life know the inspiration which we derive from their virtue, their counsel, their tenderness, and—but too often—from their compassion and their forgiveness. There is, I doubt not, still left in England many a man with chivalry and patriotism enough to challenge the world to show so perfect a specimen of humanity as a cultivated British woman.

But just because a cultivated British woman is so perfect a personage; therefore I wish to see all British women cultivated. Because the womanhood of England is so precious a treasure; I wish to see none of it wasted. It is an invaluable capital, or material, out of which the greatest possible profit to the nation must be made. And that can only be done by Thrift; and that, again, can only be attained by knowledge.

Consider that word Thrift. If you will look at "Dr. Johnson's Dictionary," or if you know your "Shakespeare," you will see that Thrift signified originally profits, gain, riches gotten—in a word, the marks of a man's thriving.

How, then, did the word Thrift get to mean parsimony, frugality, the opposite of waste? Just in the same way as economy—which first, of course, meant the management of a household—got to mean also the opposite of waste.

It was found that in commerce, in husbandry, in any process, in fact, men throve in proportion as they saved their capital, their material, their force.

Now this is a great law which runs through life; one of those laws of nature—call them, rather, laws of God—which apply not merely to political economy, to commerce, and to mechanics; but to physiology, to society; to the intellect, to the heart, of every person in this room.

The secret of thriving is thrift; saving of force; to get as much work as possible done with the least expenditure of power, the least jar and obstruction, least wear and tear.

And the secret of thrift is knowledge. In proportion as you know the laws and nature of a subject, you will be able to work at it easily, surely, rapidly, successfully; instead of wasting your money or your energies in mistaken schemes, irregular efforts, which end in disappointment and exhaustion.

The secret of thrift, I say, is knowledge. The more you know, the more you can save yourself and that which belongs to you; and can do more work with less effort.

A knowledge of the laws of commercial credit, we all know, saves capital, enabling a less capital to do the work of a greater. Knowledge of the electric tele-graph saves time; knowledge of writing saves human speech and locomotion; knowledge of domestic econ-omy saves income; knowledge of sanitary laws saves health and life; knowledge of the laws of the intellect saves wear and tear of brain; and knowledge of the laws of the spirit—what does it not save?

A well-educated moral sense, a well-regulated character, saves from idleness and ennui, alternating with sentimentality and excitement, those tenderer emotions, those deeper passions, those nobler aspira-tions of humanity, which are the heritage of the wom-an far more than of the man; and which are potent in her, for evil or for good, in proportion as they are left to run wild and undisciplined; or are trained and developed into graceful, harmonious, self-restraining strength, beautiful in themselves, and a blessing to all who come under their influence.

What, therefore, I recommend to ladies in this lec-ture is thrift: thrift of themselves and of their own powers: and knowledge as the parent of thrift.

And because it is well to begin with the lower ap-plications of thrift, and to work up to the higher, I am much pleased to hear that the first course of the proposed lectures to women in this place will be one on domestic economy.

I presume that the learned gentleman who will deliver these lectures will be the last to mean by that term the mere saving of money; that he will tell you, as—being a German—he will have good reason to know, that the young lady who learns thrift in domestic economy is also learning thrift of the very highest faculties of her immortal spirit. He will tell you, I doubt not—for he must know—how you may see in Germany young ladies living in what we more luxurious British would consider something like poverty; cooking, waiting at table, and performing many a household office which would be here considered menial; and yet finding time for a cultivation of the intellect, which is, unfortunately, too rare in Great Britain.

The truth is, that we British are too wealthy. We make money, if not too rapidly for the good of the nation at large, yet too rapidly, I fear, for the good of the daughters of those who make it. Their temptation—I do not, of course, say they all yield to it—but their temptation is, to waste of the very simplest—I had almost said, if I may be pardoned the expression, of the most barbaric—kind; to an oriental waste of money, and waste of time; to a fondness for mere finery, pardonable enough, but still a waste; and to the mistaken fancy that it is the mark of a lady to sit idle and let servants do everything for her.

But it is not of this sort of waste of which I wish to speak to-day. I only mention the matter in passing, to show that high intellectual culture is not incompatible with the performance of homely household duties, and that the moral success of which I spoke just now need not be injured, any more than it is in Germany, by intellectual success likewise. I trust that these words may reassure those parents, if any such there be here, who may fear that these lectures will withdraw women from their existing sphere of interest and activity. That they should entertain such a fear is not surprising, after the extravagant opinions and schemes which have been lately broached in various quarters.

The programme to these lectures expressly disclaims any such intentions; and I, as a husband and a father, expressly disclaim any such intention likewise.

"To fit women for the more enlightened performance of their special duties;" to help them towards learning how to do better what we doubt not many of them are already doing well; is, I honestly believe, the only object of the promoters of this scheme.

Let us see now how some of these special duties can be better performed by help of a little enlightenment as to the laws which regulate them.

Now, no man will deny—certainly no man who is past forty-five, and whose digestion is beginning to quail before the lumps of beef and mutton which are the boast of a British kitchen, and to prefer, with Justice Shallow, and, I presume, Sir John Falstaff also, "any pretty little tiny kickshaws"—no man, I say, who has reached that age, but will feel it a practical comfort to him to know that the young ladies of his family are at all events good cooks; and understand, as the French do, thrift in the matter of food.

Neither will any parent who wishes, naturally enough, that his daughters should cost him as little as possible; and wishes, naturally enough also, that they should be as well dressed as possible, deny that it would be a good thing for them to be practical milliners and mantua-makers; and, by making their own clothes gracefully and well, exercise thrift in clothing.

But, beside this thrift in clothing, I am not alone, I believe, in wishing for some thrift in the energy which produces it. Labour misapplied, you will agree, is labour wasted; and as dress, I presume, is intended to adorn the person of the wearer, the making a dress which only disfigures her may be considered as a plain case of waste. It would be impertinent in me to go into any details: but it is impossible to walk about the streets now without passing young people who must be under a deep delusion as to the success of their own toilette. Instead of graceful and noble simplicity of form, instead of combinations of colour at once rich and delicate, because in accordance with the chromatic laws of nature, one meets with phenomena more and more painful to the eye, and startling to common sense, till one would be hardly more astonished, and certainly hardly more shocked, if in a year or two, one should pass someone going about like a Chinese lady, with pinched feet, or like a savage of the Amazons, with a wooden bung through her lower lip. It is easy to complain of these monstrosities: but impossible to cure them, it seems to me, without an education of the taste, an education in those laws of nature which produce beauty in form and beauty in colour. For that the cause of these failures lies in want of education is patent. They are most common in—I had almost said they are confined to—those classes of well-to-do persons who are the least educated; who have no standard of taste of their own; and who do not acquire any from cultivated friends and relations: who, in consequence, dress themselves blindly according to what they conceive to be the Paris fashions, conveyed at third-hand through an equally uneducated dress-maker; in innocent ignorance of the fact—for fact I believe it to be—that Paris fashions are invented now not in the least for the sake of beauty, but for the sake of producing, through variety, increased expenditure, and thereby increased employment; according to the strange system which now prevails in France of com-pelling, if not prosperity, at least the signs of it; and like schoolboys before a holiday, nailing up the head of the weather-glass to insure fine weather.

Let British ladies educate themselves in those laws of beauty which are as eternal as any other of nature's laws; which may be seen fulfilled, as Mr. Ruskin tells us, so eloquently in every flower and every leaf, in ev-ery sweeping down and rippling wave; and they will be able to invent graceful and economical dresses for themselves, without importing tawdry and expensive ugliness from France.

Let me now go a step farther, and ask you to con-sider this: There are in England now a vast number, and an increasing number, of young women who, from various circumstances which we all know, must in after life be either the mistresses of their own fortunes, or the earners of their own bread. And, to do that wisely and well, they must be more or less women of business, and to be women of business they must know something of the meaning of the words Capital, Profit, Price, Value, Labour, Wages, and of the relation between those two last. In a word, they must know a little political economy. Nay, I sometimes think that the mistress of every household might find, not only thrift of money, but thrift of brain; freedom from mistakes, anxieties, worries of many kinds, all of which eat out the health as well as the heart, by a little sound knowledge of the principles of political economy.

When we consider that every mistress of a household is continually buying, if not selling; that she is continually hiring and employing labour in the form of servants; and very often, into the bargain, keeping her husband's accounts: I cannot but think that her hard-worked brain might be clearer, and her hard-tried desire to do her duty by every subject in her little kingdom, might be more easily satisfied, had she read something of what Mr. John Stuart Mill has written, especially on the duties of employer and employed. A capitalist, a commercialist, an employer of labour, and an accountant—every mistress of a household is all these, whether she likes it or not; and it would be surely well for her, in so very complicated a state of society as this, not to trust merely to that mother-wit, that intuitive sagacity and innate power of ruling her fellow-creatures, which carries women so nobly through their work in simpler and less civilised societies.

And here I stop to answer those who may say—as I have heard it said—That a woman's intellect is not fit for business; that when a woman takes to business, she is apt to do it ill, and unpleasantly likewise, to be more suspicious, more irritable, more grasping, more unreasonable, than regular men of business would be: that—as I have heard it put—"a woman does not fight fair." The answer is simple. That a woman's intellect is eminently fitted for business is proved by the enormous amount of business she gets through without any special training for it: but those faults in a woman of which some men complain are simply the results of her not having had a special training. She does not know the laws of business. She does not know the rules of the game she is playing; and therefore she is playing it in the dark, in fear and suspicion, apt to judge of questions on personal grounds, often offending those with whom she has to do, and oftener still making herself miserable over matters of law or of business, on which a little sound knowledge would set her head and her heart at rest.

When I have seen widows, having the care of children, of a great household, of a great estate, of a great business, struggling heroically, and yet often mistakenly; blamed severely for selfishness and ambition, while they were really sacrificing themselves with the divine instinct of a mother for their children's interest: I have stood by with mingled admiration and pity, and said to myself: "How nobly she is doing the work without teaching! How much more nobly would she have done it had she been taught! She is now doing her work at the most enormous waste of energy and of virtue: had she had knowledge, thrift would have followed it; she would have done more work with far less trouble. She will probably kill herself if she goes on; while sound knowledge would have saved her health, saved her heart, saved her friends, and helped the very loved ones for whom she labours, not always with success."

A little political economy, therefore, will at least do no harm to a woman; especially if she have to take care of herself in after life; neither, I think, will she be much harmed by some sound knowledge of another subject, which I see promised in these lectures: "Natural philosophy, in its various branches, such as the chemistry of common life, light, heat, electricity, etc. etc."

A little knowledge of the laws of light, for instance, would teach many women that by shutting themselves up day after day, week after week, in darkened rooms, they are as certainly committing a waste of health, destroying their vital energy, and diseasing their brains, as if they were taking so much poison the whole time.

A little knowledge of the laws of heat would teach women not to clothe themselves and their children after foolish and insufficient fashions, which in this climate sow the seeds of a dozen different diseases, and have to be atoned for by perpetual anxieties, and by perpetual doctors' bills; and as for a little knowledge of the laws of electricity, one thrift I am sure it would produce—thrift to us men, of having to answer continual inquiries as to what the weather is going to be, when a slight knowledge of the barometer, or of the form of the clouds and the direction of the wind, would enable many a lady to judge for herself, and not, after inquiry on inquiry, regardless of all warnings, go out on the first appearance of a strip of blue sky, and come home wet through, with what she calls "only a chill," but which really means a nail driven into her coffin—a probable shortening, though it may be a very small one, of her mortal life; because the food of the next twenty-four hours, which should have gone to keep the vital heat at its normal standard, will have to be wasted in raising it up to that standard, from which it has fallen by a chill.

Ladies, these are subjects on which I must beg to speak a little more at length, premising them by one statement, which may seem jest, but is solemn earnest—that, if the medical men of this or any other city were what the world now calls "alive to their own interests"—that is, to the mere making of money; instead of being, what medical men are, the most generous, disinterested, and high-minded class in these realms, then they would oppose by all means in their power the delivery of lectures on natural philosophy to women. For if women act upon what they learn in those lectures—and having women's hearts, they will act upon it—there ought to follow a decrease of sickness and an increase of health, especially among children; a thrift of life, and a thrift of expense besides, which would very seriously affect the income of medical men.

For let me ask you, ladies, with all courtesy, but with all earnestness—Are you aware of certain facts, of which every one of those excellent medical men is too well aware? Are you aware that more human beings are killed in England every year by unnecessary and preventable diseases than were killed at Waterloo or at Sadowa? Are you aware that the great majority of those victims are children? Are you aware that the diseases which carry them off are for the most part such as ought to be specially under the control of the women who love them, pet them, educate them, and would in many cases, if need be, lay down their lives for them? Are you aware, again, of the vast amount of disease which, so both wise mothers and wise doctors assure me, is engendered in the sleeping-room from simple ignorance of the laws of ventilation, and in the schoolroom likewise, from simple ignorance of the laws of physiology? from an ignorance of which I shall mention no other case here save one—that too often from ignorance of signs of approaching disease, a child is punished for what is called idleness, listlessness, wilfulness, sulkiness; and punished, too, in the unwisest way—by an increase of tasks and confinement to the house, thus overtasking still more a brain already overtasked, and depressing still more, by robbing it of oxygen and of exercise, a system already depressed? Are you aware, I ask again, of all this? I speak earnest upon this point, because I speak with experience. As a single instance: a medical man, a friend of mine, passing by his own schoolroom, heard one of his own little girls screaming and crying, and went in. The governess, an excellent woman, but wholly ignorant of the laws of physiology, complained that the child had of late become obstinate and would not learn; and that therefore she must punish her by keeping her indoors over the unlearnt lessons. The father, who knew that the child was usually a very good one, looked at her carefully for a little while; sent her out of the schoolroom; and then said, "That child must not open a book for a month." "If I had not acted so," he said to me, "I should have had that child dead of brain-disease within the year."

Now, in the face of such facts as these, is it too much to ask of mothers, sisters, aunts, nurses, governesses— all who may be occupied in the care of children, especially of girls—that they should study thrift of human health and human life, by studying somewhat the laws of life and health? There are books—I may say a whole literature of books—written by scientific doctors on these matters, which are in my mind far more important to the schoolroom than half the trashy accomplishments, so-called, which are expected to be known by governesses. But are they bought? Are they even to be bought, from most country booksellers? Ah, for a little knowledge of the laws to the neglect of which is owing so much fearful disease, which, if it does not produce immediate death, too often leaves the constitution impaired for years to come. Ah the waste of health and strength in the young; the waste, too, of anxiety and misery in those who love and tend them. How much of it might be saved by a little rational education in those laws of nature which are the will of God about the welfare of our bodies, and which, therefore, we are as much bound to know and to obey, as we are bound to know and obey the spiritual laws whereon depends the welfare of our souls.

Pardon me, ladies, if I have given a moment's pain to anyone here: but I appeal to every medical man in the room whether I have not spoken the truth; and having such an opportunity as this, I felt that I must speak for the sake of children, and of women likewise, or else for ever hereafter hold my peace.

Let me pass on from this painful subject—for painful it has been to me for many years—to a question of intellectual thrift—by which I mean just now thrift of words; thrift of truth; restraint of the tongue; accuracy and modesty in statement.

Mothers complain to me that girls are apt to be—not intentionally untruthful—but exaggerative, prejudiced, incorrect, in repeating a conversation or describing an event; and that from this fault arise, as is to be expected, misunderstandings, quarrels, rumours, slanders, scandals, and what not.

Now, for this waste of words there is but one cure: and if I be told that it is a natural fault of women; that they cannot take the calm judicial view of matters which men boast, and often boast most wrongly, that they can take; that under the influence of hope, fear, delicate antipathy, honest moral indignation, they will let their eyes and ears be governed by their feelings; and see and hear only what they wish to see and hear—I answer, that it is not for me as a man to start such a theory; but that if it be true, it is an additional argument for some education which will correct this supposed natural defect. And I say deliberately that there is but one sort of education which will correct it; one which will teach young women to observe facts accurately, judge them calmly, and describe them carefully, without adding or distorting: and that is, some training in natural science.

I beg you not to be startled: but if you are, then test the truth of my theory by playing to-night at the game called "Russian Scandal;" in which a story, repeated in secret by one player to the other, comes out at the end of the game, owing to the inaccurate and—forgive me if I say it—uneducated brains through which it has passed, utterly unlike its original; not only ludicrously maimed and distorted, but often with the most fantastic additions of events, details, names, dates, places, which each player will aver that he received from the player before him. I am afraid that too much of the average gossip of every city, town, and village is little more than a game of "Russian Scandal;" with this difference that while one is but a game, the other is but too mischievous earnest.

But now, if among your party there shall be an average lawyer, medical man, or man of science, you will find that he, and perhaps he alone, will be able to retail accurately the story which has been told him. And why? Simply because his mind has been trained to deal with facts; to ascertain exactly what he does see or hear, and to imprint its leading features strongly and clearly on his memory.

Now, you certainly cannot make young ladies barristers or attorneys; nor employ their brains in getting up cases, civil or criminal; and as for chemistry, they and their parents may have a reasonable antipathy to smells, blackened fingers, and occasional explosions and poisonings. But you may make them something of botanists, zoologists, geologists.

I could say much on this point: allow me at least to say this: I verify believe that any young lady who would employ some of her leisure time in collecting wild flowers, carefully examining them, verifying them, and arranging them; or who would in her summer trip to the sea-coast do the same by the common objects of the shore, instead of wasting her holiday, as one sees hundreds doing, in lounging on benches on the esplanade, reading worthless novels, and criticising dresses—that such a young lady, I say, would not only open her own mind to a world of wonder, beauty, and wisdom, which, if it did not make her a more reverent and pious soul, she cannot be the woman which I take for granted she is; but would save herself from the habit—I had almost said the necessity—of gossip; because she would have things to think of and not merely persons; facts instead of fancies; while she would acquire something of accuracy, of patience, of methodical observation and judgment, which would stand her in good stead in the events of daily life, and increase her power of bridling her tongue and her imagination. "God is in heaven, and thou upon earth; therefore let thy words be few;" is the lesson which those are learning all day long who study the works of God with reverent accuracy, lest by misrepresenting them they should be tempted to say that God has done that which He has not; and in that wholesome discipline I long that women as well as men should share.

And now I come to a thrift of the highest kind, as contrasted with a waste the most deplorable and ruinous of all; thrift of those faculties which connect us with the unseen and spiritual world; with humanity, with Christ, with God; thrift of the immortal spirit. I am not going now to give you a sermon on duty. You hear such, I doubt not, in church every Sunday, far better than I can preach to you. I am going to speak rather of thrift of the heart, thrift of the emotions. How they are wasted in these days in reading what are called sensation novels, all know but too well; how British literature—all that the best hearts and intellects among our forefathers have bequeathed to us—is neglected for light fiction, the reading of which is, as a lady well said, "the worst form of intemperance—dram-drinking and opium-eating, intellectual and moral."

I know that the young will delight—they have delighted in all ages, and will to the end of time—in fictions which deal with that "oldest tale which is for ever new." Novels will be read: but that is all the more reason why women should be trained, by the perusal of a higher, broader, deeper literature, to distinguish the good novel from the bad, the moral from the immoral, the noble from the base, the true work of art from the sham which hides its shallowness and vulgarity under a tangled plot and melodramatic situations. She should learn—and that she can only learn by cultivation—to discern with joy, and drink in with reverence, the good, the beautiful, and the true; and to turn with the fine scorn of a pure and strong womanhood from the bad, the ugly, and the false.

And if any parent should be inclined to reply: "Why lay so much stress upon educating a girl in British literature? Is it not far more important to make our daughters read religious books?" I answer—Of course it is. I take for granted that that is done in a Christian land. But I beg you to recollect that there are books and books; and that in these days of a free press it is impossible, in the long run, to prevent girls reading books of very different shades of opinion, and very different religious worth. It may be, therefore, of the very highest importance to a girl to have her intellect, her taste, her emotions, her moral sense, in a word, her whole womanhood, so cultivated and regulated that she shall herself be able to discern the true from the false, the orthodox from the unorthodox, the truly devout from the merely sentimental, the Gospel from its counterfeits.

I should have thought that there never had been in Britain, since the Reformation, a crisis at which young Englishwomen required more careful cultivation on these matters; if at least they are to be saved from making themselves and their families miserable; and from ending—as I have known too many end—with broken hearts, broken brains, broken health, and an early grave.

Take warning by what you see abroad. In every country where the women are uneducated, unoccupied; where their only literature is French novels or translations of them—in every one of those countries the women, even to the highest, are the slaves of superstition, and the puppets of priests. In proportion as, in certain other countries—notably, I will say, in Scotland—the women are highly educated, family life and family secrets are sacred, and the woman owns allegiance and devotion to no confessor or director, but to her own husband or to her own family.

I say plainly, that if any parents wish their daughters to succumb at least to some quackery or superstition, whether calling itself scientific, or calling itself religious—and there are too many of both just now— they cannot more certainly effect their purpose than by allowing her to grow up ignorant, frivolous, luxurious, vain; with her emotions excited, but not satisfied, by the reading of foolish and even immoral novels.

In such a case the more delicate and graceful the organisation, the more noble and earnest the nature, which has been neglected, the more certain it is—I know too well what I am saying—to go astray.

The time of depression, disappointment, vacuity, all but despair must come. The immortal spirit, finding no healthy satisfaction for its highest aspirations, is but too likely to betake itself to an unhealthy and exciting superstition. Ashamed of its own long self-indulgence, it is but too likely to flee from itself into a morbid asceticism. Not having been taught its God-given and natural duties in the world, it is but too likely to betake itself, from the mere craving for action, to self-invented and unnatural duties out of the world. Ignorant of true science, yet craving to understand the wonders of nature and of spirit, it is but too likely to betake itself to non-science—nonsense as it is usually called—whether of spirit-rapping and mesmerism, or of miraculous relics and winking pictures. Longing for guidance and teaching, and never having been taught to guide and teach itself, it is but too likely to deliver itself up in self-despair to the guidance and teaching of those who, whether they be quacks or fanatics, look on uneducated women as their natural prey.

You will see, I am sure, from what I have said, that it is not my wish that you should become mere learned women; mere female pedants, as useless and unpleasing as male pedants are wont to be. The education which I set before you is not to be got by mere hearing lectures or reading books: for it is an education of your whole character; a self-education; which really means a committing of yourself to God, that He may educate you. Hearing lectures is good, for it will teach you how much there is to be known, and how little you know. Reading books is good, for it will give you habits of regular and diligent study. And therefore I urge on you strongly private study, especially in case a library should be formed here of books on those most practical subjects of which I have been speaking. But, after all, both lectures and books are good, mainly in as far as they furnish matter for reflection: while the desire to reflect and the ability to reflect must come, as I believe, from above. The honest craving after light and power, after knowledge, wisdom, active usefulness, must come—and may it come to you—by the inspiration of the Spirit of God.

One word more, and I have done. Let me ask women to educate themselves, not for their own sakes merely, but for the sake of others. For, whether they will or not, they must educate others. I do not speak merely of those who may be engaged in the work of direct teaching; that they ought to be well taught themselves, who can doubt? I speak of those—and in so doing I speak of every woman, young and old— who exercise as wife, as mother, as aunt, as sister, or as friend, an influence, indirect it may be, and unconscious, but still potent and practical, on the minds and characters of those about them, especially of men. How potent and practical that influence is, those know best who know most of the world and most of human nature. There are those who con- sider—and I agree with them—that the education of boys under the age of twelve years ought to be entrusted as much as possible to women. Let me ask—of what period of youth and manhood does not the same hold true? I pity the ignorance and conceit of the man who fancies that he has nothing left to learn from cultivated women. I should have thought that the very mission of woman was to be, in the highest sense, the educator of man from infancy to old age; that that was the work towards which all the God-given capacities of women pointed; for which they were to be educated to the highest pitch. I should have thought that it was the glory of woman that she was sent into the world to live for others, rather than for herself; and therefore I should say—Let her smallest rights be respected, her smallest wrongs redressed: but let her never be persuaded to forget that she is sent into the world to teach man—what, I believe, she has been teaching him all along, even in the savage state—namely, that there is something more necessary than the claiming of rights, and that is, the performing of duties; to teach him specially, in these so-called intellectual days, that there is something more than intellect, and that is—purity and virtue. Let her never be persuaded to forget that her calling is not the lower and more earthly one of self-assertion, but the higher and the diviner calling of self-sacrifice; and let her never desert that higher life, which lives in others and for others, like her Redeemer and her Lord.

And if any should answer that this doctrine would keep woman a dependent and a slave, I rejoin—Not so: it would keep her what she should be—the mistress of all around her, because mistress of herself. And more, I should express a fear that those who made that answer had not yet seen into the mystery of true greatness and true strength; that they did not yet understand the true magnanimity, the true royalty of that spirit, by which the Son of man came not to be ministered unto, but to minister, and to give His life a ransom for many.

Surely that is woman's calling—to teach man: and to teach him what? To teach him, after all, that his calling is the same as hers, if he will but see the things which belong to his peace. To temper his fiercer, coarser, more self-assertive nature, by the contact of her gentleness, purity, self-sacrifice. To make him see that not by blare of trumpets, not by noise, wrath, greed, ambition, intrigue, puffery, is good and lasting work to be done on earth: but by wise self-distrust, by silent labour, by lofty self-control, by that charity which hopeth all things, believeth all things, endureth all things; by such an example, in short, as women now in tens of thousands set to those around them; such as they will show more and more, the more their whole womanhood is educated to employ its powers without waste and without haste in harmonious unity. Let the woman begin in girlhood, if such be her happy lot— to quote the words of a great poet, a great philosopher, and a great Churchman, William Wordsworth—let her begin, I say—

> *With all things round about her drawn*
> *From May-time and the cheerful dawn;*
> *A dancing shape, an image gay,*
> *To haunt, to startle, and waylay.*

Let her develop onwards—

> *A spirit, yet a woman too,*
> *With household motions light and free,*
> *And steps of virgin liberty.*
> *A countenance in which shall meet*
> *Sweet records, promises as sweet;*
> *A creature not too bright and good*
> *For human nature's daily food;*
> *For transient sorrows, simple wiles,*
> *Praise, blame, love, kisses, tears, and smiles.*

But let her highest and her final development be that which not nature, but self-education alone can bring—that which makes her once and for ever—

> *A being breathing thoughtful breath;*
> *A traveller betwixt life and death.*
> *With reason firm, with temperate will*
> *Endurance, foresight, strength, and skill.*
> *A perfect woman, nobly planned,*
> *To warn, to comfort, and command.*
> *And yet a spirit still and bright*
> *With something of an angel light.*

NAUSICAA IN LONDON;
OR, THE LOWER EDUCATION OF WOMEN

Fresh from the Marbles of the British Museum, I went my way through London streets. My brain was still full of fair and grand forms; the forms of men and women whose every limb and attitude betokened perfect health, and grace, and power, and self-possession and self-restraint so habitual and complete that it had become unconscious, and undistinguishable from the native freedom of the savage. For I had been up and down the corridors of those Greek sculptures, which remain as a perpetual sermon to rich and poor, amid our artificial, unwholesome, and it may be decaying pseudo-civilisation, saying with looks more expressive than all words—Such men and women can be; for such they have been; and such you may be yet, if you will use that science of which you too often only boast. Above all, I had been pondering over the awful and yet tender beauty of the maiden figures from the Parthenon and its kindred temples. And these, or such as these, I thought to myself, were the sisters of the men who fought at Marathon and Salamis;

the mothers of many a man among the ten thousand whom Xenophon led back from Babylon to the Black Sea shore; the ancestresses of many a man who conquered the East in Alexander's host, and fought with Porus in the far Punjab. And were these women mere dolls? These men mere gladiators? Were they not the parents of philosophy, science, poetry, the plastic arts? We talk of education now. Are we more educated than were the ancient Greeks? Do we know anything about education, physical, intellectual, or æsthetic, and I may say moral likewise—religious education, of course, in our sense of the world, they had none—but do we know anything about education of which they have not taught us at least the rudiments? Are there not some branches of education which they perfected, once and for ever; leaving us northern barbarians to follow, or else not to follow, their example? To produce health, that is, harmony and sympathy, proportion and grace, in every faculty of mind and body—that was their notion of education. To produce that, the text-book of their childhood was the poetry of Homer, and not of—But I am treading on dangerous ground. It was for this that the seafaring Greek lad was taught to find his ideal in Ulysses; while his sister at home found hers, it may be, in Nausicaa. It was for this, that when perhaps the most complete and exquisite of all the Greeks, Sophocles the good, beloved by gods and men, represented on the Athenian stage his drama of Nausicaa, and, as usual, could not—for he had no voice—himself take a speaking part, he was content to do one thing in which he specially excelled; and dressed and masked as a girl, to play at ball amid the chorus of Nausicaa's maidens.

That drama of Nausicaa is lost; and if I dare say so of any play of Sophocles', I scarce regret it. It is well, perhaps, that we have no second conception of the scene, to interfere with the simplicity, so grand, and yet so tender, of Homer's idyllic episode.

Nausicaa, it must be remembered, is the daughter of a king. But not of a king in the exclusive modern European or old Eastern sense. Her father, Alcinous, is simply primus inter pares among a community of merchants, who are called "kings" likewise; and Mayor for life—so to speak—of a new trading city, a nascent Genoa or Venice, on the shore of the Mediterranean. But the girl Nausicaa, as she sleeps in her "carved chamber," is "like the immortals in form and face;" and two handmaidens who sleep on each side of the polished door "have beauty from the Graces."

To her there enters, in the shape of some maiden friend, none less than Pallas Athene herself, intent on saving worthily her favourite, the shipwrecked Ulysses; and bids her in a dream go forth—and wash the clothes.[6]

Nausicaa, wherefore doth thy mother bear
Child so forgetful? This long time doth rest,
Like lumber in the house, much raiment fair.
Soon must thou wed, and be thyself well-drest,

---

6 I quote from the translation of the late lamented Philip Stanhope Worsley, of Corpus Christi College, Oxford.

And find thy bridegroom raiment of the best.
These are the things whence good repute is born,
And praises that make glad a parent's breast.
Come, let us both go washing with the morn;
So shalt thou have clothes becoming to be worn.

Know that thy maidenhood is not for long,
Whom the Phoeacian chiefs already woo,
Lords of the land whence thou thyself art sprung.
Soon as the shining dawn comes forth anew,
For wain and mules thy noble father sue,
Which to the place of washing shall convey
Girdles and shawls and rugs of splendid hue,
This for thyself were better than essay
Thither to walk: the place is distant a long way.

Startled by her dream, Nausicaa awakes, and goes to find her parents—

One by the hearth sat, with the maids around,
And on the skeins of yarn, sea-purpled, spent
Her morning toil. Him to the council bound,
Called by the honoured kings, just going forth she found.

And calling him, as she might now, Pappa phile, Dear Papa, asks for the mule-waggon: but it is her father's and her five brothers' clothes she fain would wash,—

Ashamed to name her marriage to her father dear.

But he understood all—and she goes forth in the mule-waggon, with the clothes, after her mother has put in "a chest of all kinds of delicate food, and meat, and wine in a goatskin;" and last but not least, the in-dispensable cruse of oil for anointing after the bath, to which both Jews, Greeks, and Romans owed so much health and beauty. And then we read in the simple verse of a poet too refined, like the rest of his race, to see anything mean or ridiculous in that which was not ugly and unnatural, how she and her maids got into the "polished waggon," "with good wheels," and she "took the whip and the studded reins," and "beat them till they started;" and how the mules, "rattled" away, and "pulled against each other," till

> When they came to the fair flowing river
> Which feeds good lavatories all the year,
> Fitted to cleanse all sullied robes soever,
> They from the wain the mules unharnessed there,
> And chased them free, to crop their juicy fare
> By the swift river, on the margin green;
> Then to the waters dashed the clothes they bare
> And in the stream-filled trenches stamped them clean.
> Which, having washed and cleansed, they spread before
> The sunbeams, on the beach, where most did lie
> Thick pebbles, by the sea-wave washed ashore.
> So, having left them in the heat to dry,
> They to the bath went down, and by-and-by,
> Rubbed with rich oil, their midday meal essay,
> Couched in green turf, the river rolling nigh.
> Then, throwing off their veils, at ball they play,
> While the white-armed Nausicaa leads the choral lay.

The mere beauty of this scene all will feel, who have the sense of beauty in them. Yet it is not on that aspect which I wish to dwell, but on its healthfulness. Exercise is taken, in measured time, to the sound of song, as a duty almost, as well as an amusement. For this game of ball, which is here mentioned for the first time in human literature, nearly three thousand years ago, was held by the Greeks and by the Romans after them, to be an almost necessary part of a liberal education; principally, doubtless, from the development which it produced in the upper half of the body, not merely to the arms, but to the chest, by raising and expanding the ribs, and to all the muscles of the torso, whether perpendicular or oblique. The elasticity and grace which it was believed to give were so much prized, that a room for ball-play, and a teacher of the art, were integral parts of every gymnasium; and the Athenians went so far as to bestow on one famous ball-player, Aristonicus of Carystia, a statue and the rights of citizenship. The rough and hardy young Spartans, when passing from boyhood into manhood, received the title of ball-players, seemingly from the game which it was then their special duty to learn. In the case of Nausicaa and her maidens, the game would just bring into their right places all that is liable to be contracted and weakened in women, so many of whose occupations must needs be sedentary and stooping; while the song which accompanied the game at once filled the lungs regularly and rhythmically, and prevented violent motion, or unseemly attitude. We, the civilised, need physiologists to remind us of these simple facts, and even then do not act on them. Those old half-barbarous Greeks had found them out for themselves, and, moreover, acted on them.

But fair Nausicaa must have been—some will say—surely a mere child of nature, and an uncultivated person?

So far from it, that her whole demeanour and speech show culture of the very highest sort, full of "sweetness and light."—Intelligent and fearless, quick to perceive the bearings of her strange and sudden adventure, quick to perceive the character of Ulysses, quick to answer his lofty and refined pleading by words as lofty and refined, and pious withal;—for it is she who speaks to her handmaids the once so famous words:

Strangers and poor men all are sent from Zeus;
And alms, though small, are sweet.

Clear of intellect, prompt of action, modest of demeanour, shrinking from the slightest breath of scandal; while she is not ashamed, when Ulysses, bathed and dressed, looks himself again, to whisper to her maidens her wish that the Gods might send her such a spouse.—This is Nausicaa as Homer draws her; and as many a scholar and poet since Homer has accepted her for the ideal of noble maidenhood. I ask my readers to study for themselves her interview with Ulysses, in Mr. Worsley's translation, or rather in the grand simplicity of the original Greek,[7] and judge wheth-

---

7   Odyssey, book vi. 127-315; vol. i. pp. 143-150 of Mr. Worsley's translation.

er Nausicaa is not as perfect a lady as the poet who imagined her—or, it may be, drew her from life—must have been a perfect gentleman; both complete in those "manners" which, says the old proverb, "make the man:" but which are the woman herself; because with her—who acts more by emotion than by calculation—manners are the outward and visible tokens of her inward and spiritual grace, or disgrace; and flow instinctively, whether good or bad, from the instincts of her inner nature.

True, Nausicaa could neither read nor write. No more, most probably, could the author of the Odyssey. No more, for that matter, could Abraham, Isaac, and Jacob, though they were plainly, both in mind and manners, most highly-cultivated men. Reading and writing, of course, have now become necessaries of humanity; and are to be given to every human being, that he may start fair in the race of life. But I am not aware that Greek women improved much, either in manners, morals, or happiness, by acquiring them in after centuries. A wise man would sooner see his daughter a Nausicaa than a Sappho, an Aspasia, a Cleopatra, or even an Hypatia.

Full of such thoughts, I went through London streets, among the Nausicaas of the present day; the girls of the period; the daughters and hereafter mothers of our future rulers, the great Demos or commercial middle class of the greatest mercantile city in the world: and noted what I had noted with fear and sorrow, many a day, for many a year; a type, and an increasing type, of young women who certainly had not had the "advantages," "educational" and other, of that Greek Nausicaa of old.

Of course, in such a city as London, to which the best of everything, physical and other, gravitates, I could not but pass, now and then, beautiful persons, who made me proud of those grandes Anglaises aux joues rouges, whom the Parisiennes ridicule—and envy. But I could not help suspecting that their looks showed them to be either country-bred, or born of country parents; and this suspicion was strengthened by the fact that, when compared with their mothers, the mother's physique was, in the majority of cases, superior to the daughters'. Painful it was, to one accustomed to the ruddy well-grown peasant girl, stalwart, even when, as often, squat and plain, to remark the exceedingly small size of the average young woman; by which I do not mean mere want of height—that is a little matter—but want of breadth likewise; a general want of those large frames, which indicate usually a power of keeping strong and healthy not merely the muscles, but the brain itself.

Poor little things. I passed hundreds—I pass hundreds every day—trying to hide their littleness by the nasty mass of false hair—or what does duty for it; and by the ugly and useless hat which is stuck upon it, making the head thereby look ridiculously large and heavy; and by the high heels on which they totter onward, having forgotten, or never learnt, the simple art of walking; their bodies tilted forward in that ungraceful attitude which is called—why that name of all others?—a "Grecian bend;" seemingly kept on their feet, and kept together at all, in that strange attitude, by tight stays which prevented all graceful and healthy motion of the hips or sides; their raiment, meanwhile, being purposely misshapen in this direction and in that, to hide—it must be presumed—deficiencies of form. If that chignon and those heels had been taken off, the figure which would have remained would have been that too often of a puny girl of sixteen. And yet there was no doubt that these women were not only full grown, but some of them, alas! wives and mothers.

Poor little things.—And this they have gained by so-called civilisation: the power of aping the "fashions" by which the worn-out "Parisienne" hides her own personal defects; and of making themselves, by innate want of that taste which the "Parisienne" possesses, only the cause of something like a sneer from many a cultivated man; and of something like a sneer, too, from yonder gipsy woman who passes by, with bold bright face, and swinging hip, and footstep stately and elastic; far better dressed, according to all true canons of taste, than most town-girls; and thanking her fate that she and her "Rom" are no house-dwellers and gaslight-sightseers, but fatten on free air upon the open moor.

But the face which is beneath that chignon and that hat? Well—it is sometimes pretty: but how seldom handsome, which is a higher quality by far. It is not, strange to say, a well-fed face. Plenty of money, and perhaps too much, is spent on those fine clothes.

It had been better, to judge from the complexion, if some of that money had been spent in solid wholesome food. She looks as if she lived—as she too often does, I hear—on tea and bread-and-butter, or rather on bread with the minimum of butter. For as the want of bone indicates a deficiency of phosphatic food, so does the want of flesh about the cheeks indicate a deficiency of hydrocarbon. Poor little Nausicaa:—that is not her fault. Our boasted civilisation has not even taught her what to eat, as it certainly has not increased her appetite; and she knows not—what every country fellow knows—that without plenty of butter and other fatty matters, she is not likely to keep even warm. Better to eat nasty fat bacon now, than to supply the want of it some few years hence by nastier cod-liver oil. But there is no one yet to tell her that, and a dozen other equally simple facts, for her own sake, and for the sake of that coming Demos which she is to bring into the world; a Demos which, if we can only keep it healthy in body and brain, has before it so splendid a future: but which, if body and brain degrade beneath the influence of modern barbarism, is but too likely to follow the Demos of ancient Byzantium, or of modern Paris.

Ay, but her intellect. She is so clever, and she reads so much, and she is going to be taught to read so much more.

Ah well—there was once a science called Physiognomy. The Greeks, from what I can learn, knew more of it than any people since: though the Italian painters and sculptors must have known much; far more

99

than we. In a more scientific civilisation there will be such a science once more: but its laws, though still in the empiric stage, are not altogether forgotten by some. Little children have often a fine and clear instinct of them. Many cultivated and experienced women have a fine and clear instinct of them likewise. And some such would tell us that there is intellect in plenty in the modern Nausicaa: but not of the quality which they desire for their country's future good. Self-consciousness, eagerness, volubility, petulance in countenance, in gesture, and in voice—which last is too often most harsh and artificial, the breath being sent forth through the closed teeth, and almost entirely at the corners of the mouth—and, with all this, a weariness often about the wrinkling forehead and the drooping lids;—all these, which are growing too common, not among the Demos only, nor only in the towns, are signs, they think, of the unrest of unhealth, physical, intellectual, spiritual. At least they are as different as two types of physiognomy in the same race can be, from the expression both of face and gesture, in those old Greek sculptures, and in the old Italian painters; and, it must be said, in the portraits of Reynolds, and Gainsborough, Copley, and Romney. Not such, one thinks, must have been the mothers of Britain during the latter half of the last century and the beginning of the present; when their sons, at times, were holding half the world at bay.

And if Nausicaa has become such in town: what is she when she goes to the seaside, not to wash the clothes in fresh-water, but herself in salt—the very salt-water, laden with decaying organisms, from which, though not polluted further by a dozen sewers, Ulysses had to cleanse himself, anointing, too, with oil, ere he was fit to appear in the company of Nausicaa of Greece? She dirties herself with the dirty salt-water; and probably chills and tires herself by walking thither and back, and staying in too long; and then flaunts on the pier, bedizened in garments which, for monstrosity of form and disharmony of colours, would have set that Greek Nausicaa's teeth on edge, or those of any average Hindoo woman now. Or, even sadder still, she sits on chairs and benches all the weary afternoon, her head drooped on her chest, over some novel from the "Library;" and then returns to tea and shrimps, and lodgings of which the fragrance is not unsuggestive, sometimes not unproductive, of typhoid fever. Ah, poor Nausicaa of England! That is a sad sight to some who think about the present, and have read about the past. It is not a sad sight to see your old father—tradesman, or clerk, or what not—who has done good work in his day, and hopes to do some more, sitting by your old mother, who has done good work in her day—among the rest, that heaviest work of all, the bringing you into the world and keeping you in it till now—honest, kindly, cheerful folk enough, and not inefficient in their own calling; though an average Northumbrian, or Highlander, or Irish Easterling, beside carrying a brain of five times the intellectual force, could drive five such men over the cliff with his bare hands. It is not a sad sight, I say, to see them sitting about upon those seaside benches, looking out listlessly at the water, and the ships, and the sunlight, and enjoying, like so many flies upon a wall, the novel act of doing nothing. It is not the old for whom wise men are sad: but for you. Where is your vitality? Where is your "Lebens-gluckseligkeit," your enjoyment of superfluous life and power? Why you cannot even dance and sing, till now and then, at night, perhaps, when you ought to lie safe in bed, but when the weak brain, after receiving the day's nourishment, has roused itself a second time into a false excitement of gaslight pleasure. What there is left of it is all going into that foolish book, which the womanly element in you, still healthy and alive, delights in; because it places you in fancy in situations in which you will never stand, and inspires you with emotions, some of which, it may be, you had better never feel. Poor Nausicaa—old, some men think, before you have been ever young.

And now they are going to "develop" you; and let you have your share in "the higher education of women," by making you read more books, and do more sums, and pass examinations, and stoop over desks at night after stooping over some other employment all day; and to teach you Latin, and even Greek!

Well, we will gladly teach you Greek, if you learn thereby to read the history of Nausicaa of old, and what manner of maiden she was, and what was her education. You will admire her, doubtless. But do not let your admiration limit itself to drawing a

meagre half-mediaevalised design of her—as she never looked. Copy in your own person; and even if you
do not descend as low—or rise as high—as washing
the household clothes, at least learn to play at ball;
and sing, in the open air and sunshine, not in theatres and concert-rooms by gaslight; and take decent
care of your own health; and dress not like a "Parisienne"—nor, of course, like Nausicaa of old, for that is
to ask too much:—but somewhat more like an average Highland lassie; and try to look like her, and be
like her, of whom Wordsworth sang:

A mien and face
In which full plainly I can trace
Benignity, and home-bred sense,
Ripening in perfect innocence.
Here scattered, like a random seed,
Remote from men, thou dost not need
The embarrassed look of shy distress
And maidenly shamefacedness.
Thou wear'st upon thy forehead clear
The freedom of a mountaineer.
A face with gladness overspread,
Soft smiles, by human kindness bred,
And seemliness complete, that sways
Thy courtesies, about thee plays.
With no restraint, save such as springs
From quick and eager visitings
Of thoughts that lie beyond the reach
Of thy few words of English speech.
A bondage sweetly brooked, a strife
That gives thy gestures grace and life.

Ah, yet unspoilt Nausicaa of the North; descendant of the dark tender-hearted Celtic girl, and the fair deep-hearted Scandinavian Viking, thank God for thy heather and fresh air, and the kine thou tendest, and the wool thou spinnest; and come not to seek thy fortune, child, in wicked London town; nor import, as they tell me thou art doing fast, the ugly fashions of that London town, clumsy copies of Parisian cockneydom, into thy Highland home; nor give up the healthful and graceful, free and modest dress of thy mother and thy mother's mother, to disfigure the little kirk on Sabbath days with crinoline and corset, high-heeled boots, and other women's hair.

It is proposed, just now, to assimilate the education of girls more and more to that of boys. If that means that girls are merely to learn more lessons, and to study what their brothers are taught, in addition to what their mothers were taught; then it is to be hoped, at least by physiologists and patriots, that the scheme will sink into that limbo whither, in a free and tolerably rational country, all imperfect and ill-considered schemes are sure to gravitate. But if the proposal be a bona-fide one: then it must be borne in mind that in the Public schools of England, and in all private schools, I presume, which take their tone from them, cricket and football are more or less compulsory, being considered integral parts of an Englishman's education; and that they are likely to remain so, in spite of all reclamations: because masters and boys alike know that games do not, in the long run, interfere with a boy's work; that the same boy will very often excel in both; that the games keep him in health for his work; and the spirit with which he takes to his games when in the lower school, is a fair test of the spirit with which he will take to his work when he rises into the higher school; and that nothing is worse for a boy than to fall into that loafing, tuck-shop-haunting set, who neither play hard nor work hard, and are usually extravagant, and often vicious. Moreover, they know well that games conduce, not merely to physical, but to moral health; that in the playing-field boys acquire virtues which no books can give them; not merely daring and endurance, but, better still, temper, self-restraint, fairness, honour, unenvious approbation of another's success, and all that "give and take" of life which stand a man in such good stead when he goes forth into the world, and without which, indeed, his success is always maimed and partial.

Now: if the promoters of higher education for women will compel girls to any training analogous to our public-school games; if, for instance, they will insist on that most natural and wholesome of all exercises, dancing, in order to develop the lower half of the body; on singing, to expand the lungs and regulate the breath; and on some games—ball or what not—which will ensure that raised chest, and upright carriage, and general strength of the upper torso, without which full oxygenation of the blood, and therefore general health, is impossible; if they will sternly forbid tight stays, high heels, and all which interferes with free growth and free motion; if they will consider carefully all which has been written on the "half-time system" by Mr. Chadwick and others; and accept the certain physical law that, in order to renovate the brain day by day, the growing creature must have plenty of fresh air and play, and that the child who learns for four hours and plays for four hours, will learn more, and learn it more easily, than the child who learns for the whole eight hours; if, in short, they will teach girls not merely to understand the Greek tongue, but to copy somewhat of the Greek physical training, of that "music and gymnastic" which helped to make the cleverest race of the old world the ablest race likewise; then they will earn the gratitude of the patriot and the physiologists, by doing their best to stay the downward tendencies of the physique, and therefore ultimately of the morale, in the coming generation of English women.

I am sorry to say that, as yet, I hear of but one movement in this direction among the promoters of the "higher education of women." [8] I trust that the subject will be taken up methodically by those gifted ladies,

---

8   Since this essay was written, I have been sincerely delighted to find that my wishes had been anticipated at Girton College, near Cambridge, and previously at Hitchin, whence the college was removed: and that the wise ladies who superintend that establishment propose also that most excellent institution—a swimming-bath. A paper, moreover, read before the London Association of School-mistresses in 1866, on "Physical Exercises and Recreation for Girls," deserves all attention. May those who promote such things prosper as they deserve.

106

who have acquainted themselves, and are labouring to acquaint other women, with the first principles of health; and that they may avail to prevent the coming generations, under the unwholesome stimulant of competitive examinations, and so forth, from "developing" into so many Chinese—dwarfs—or idiots.

October, 1873.

THE AIR-MOTHERS

1869—Die Natur ist die Bewegung

Who are these who follow us softly over the moor in the autumn eve? Their wings brush and rustle in the fir-boughs, and they whisper before us and behind, as if they called gently to each other, like birds flocking homeward to their nests.

The woodpecker on the pine-stems knows them, and laughs aloud for joy as they pass. The rooks above the pasture know them, and wheel round and tumble in their play. The brown leaves on the oak trees know them, and flutter faintly, and beckon as they pass. And in the chattering of the dry leaves there is a meaning, and a cry of weary things which long for rest.

"Take us home, take us home, you soft air-mothers, now our fathers the sunbeams are grown dull. Our green summer beauty is all draggled, and our faces are grown wan and wan; and the buds, the children whom we nourished, thrust us off, ungrateful, from our seats. Waft us down, you soft air-mothers, upon your wings to the quiet earth, that we may go to our home, as all things go, and become air and sunlight once again."

And the bold young fir-seeds know them, and rattle impatient in their cones. "Blow stronger, blow fiercer, slow air-mothers, and shake us from our prisons of dead wood, that we may fly and spin away north-eastward, each on his horny wing. Help us but to touch the moorland yonder, and we will take good care of ourselves henceforth; we will dive like arrows through the heather, and drive our sharp beaks into the soil, and rise again as green trees toward the sunlight, and spread out lusty boughs."

They never think, bold fools, of what is coming to bring them low in the midst of their pride; of the reckless axe which will fell them, and the saw which will shape them into logs; and the trains which will roar and rattle over them, as they lie buried in the gravel of the way, till they are ground and rotted into powder, and dug up and flung upon the fire, that they too may return home, like all things, and become air and sunlight once again.

And the air-mothers hear their prayers, and do their bidding: but faintly; for they themselves are tired and sad.

Tired and sad are the air-mothers, and their gardens rent and wan. Look at them as they stream over the black forest, before the dim south-western sun; long lines and wreaths of melancholy grey, stained with dull yellow or dead dun. They have come far across the seas, and done many a wild deed upon their way; and now that they have reached the land, like shipwrecked sailors, they will lie down and weep till they can weep no more.

Ah, how different were those soft air-mothers when, invisible to mortal eyes, they started on their long sky-journey, five thousand miles across the sea! Out of the blazing caldron which lies between the two New Worlds, they leapt up when the great sun called them, in whirls and spouts of clear hot steam; and rushed of their own passion to the northward, while the whirling earth-ball whirled them east. So north-eastward they rushed aloft, across the gay West Indian isles, leaving below the glitter of the fly-ing-fish, and the sidelong eyes of cruel sharks; above the cane-fields and the plantain-gardens, and the co-coa-groves which fringe the shores; above the rocks which throbbed with earthquakes, and the peaks of old volcanoes, cinder-strewn; while, far beneath, the ghosts of their dead sisters hurried home upon the north-east breeze.

Wild deeds they did as they rushed onward, and struggled and fought among themselves, up and down, and round and backward, in the fury of their blind hot youth. They heeded not the tree as they snapped it, nor the ship as they whelmed it in the waves; nor the cry of the sinking sailor, nor the need of his lit-tle ones on shore; hasty and selfish even as children, and, like children, tamed by their own rage. For they tired themselves by struggling with each other, and by tearing the heavy water into waves; and their wings grew clogged with sea-spray, and soaked more and more with steam. But at last the sea grew cold beneath them, and their clear steam shrank to mist; and they saw themselves and each other wrapped in dull rain-laden clouds. Then they drew their white cloud-garments round them, and veiled themselves for very shame; and said: "We have been wild and wayward; and, alas! our pure bright youth is gone. But we will do one good deed yet ere we die, and so we shall not have lived in vain. We will glide onward to the land, and weep there; and refresh all things with soft warm rain; and make the grass grow, the buds burst; quench the thirst of man and beast, and wash the soiled world clean."

So they are wandering past us, the air-mothers, to weep the leaves into their graves; to weep the seeds into their seed-beds, and weep the soil into the plains; to get the rich earth ready for the winter, and then creep northward to the ice-world, and there die.

Weary, and still more weary, slowly and more slowly still, they will journey on far northward, across fast-chilling seas. For a doom is laid upon them, never to be still again, till they rest at the North Pole itself, the still axle of the spinning world; and sink in death around it, and become white snow-clad ghosts.

But will they live again, those chilled air-mothers? Yes, they must live again. For all things move for ever; and not even ghosts can rest. So the corpses of their sisters, piling on them from above, press them outward, press them southward toward the sun once more; across the floes and round the icebergs, weeping tears of snow and sleet, while men hate their wild harsh voices, and shrink before their bitter breath. They know not that the cold bleak snow-storms, as they hurtle from the black north-east, bear back the ghosts of the soft air-mothers, as penitents, to their father, the great sun.

But as they fly southwards, warm life thrills them, and they drop their loads of sleet and snow; and meet their young live sisters from the south, and greet them with flash and thunder-peal. And, please God, before many weeks are over, as we run Westward-Ho, we shall overtake the ghosts of these air-mothers, hurrying back toward their father, the great sun. Fresh and bright under the fresh bright heaven, they will race with us toward our home, to gain new heat, new life, new power, and set forth about their work once more. Men call them the south-west wind, those air-mothers; and their ghosts the north-east trade; and value them, and rightly, because they bear the traders out and home across the sea. But wise men, and little children, should look on them with more seeing eyes; and say, "May not these winds be living creatures? They, too, are thoughts of God, to whom all live."

For is not our life like their life? Do we not come and go as they? Out of God's boundless bosom, the fount of life, we came; through selfish, stormy youth and contrite tears—just not too late; through manhood not altogether useless; through slow and chill old age, we return from Whence we came; to the

Bosom of God once more—to go forth again, it may be, with fresh knowledge, and fresh powers, to nobler work. Amen.

Such was the prophecy which I learnt, or seemed to learn, from the south-western wind off the Atlantic, on a certain delectable evening. And it was fulfilled at night, as far as the gentle air-mothers could fulfil it, for foolish man.

There was a roaring in the woods all night;
The rain came heavily and fell in floods;
But now the sun is rising calm and bright,
The birds are singing in the distant woods;
Over his own sweet voice the stock-dove broods,
The jay makes answer as the magpie chatters,
And all the air is filled with pleasant noise of waters.

But was I a gloomy and distempered man, if, upon such a morn as that, I stood on the little bridge across a certain brook, and watched the water run, with something of a sigh? Or if, when the schoolboy beside me lamented that the floods would surely be out, and his day's fishing spoiled, I said to him—"Ah, my boy, that is a little matter. Look at what you are seeing now, and understand what barbarism and waste mean. Look at all that beautiful water which God has sent us hither off the Atlantic, without trouble or expense to us. Thousands, and tens of thousands, of gallons will run under this bridge to-day; and what shall we do with it? Nothing. And yet: think only of the mills which that water would have turned. Think how it might have kept up health and cleanliness in poor creatures packed away in the back streets of the nearest town, or even in London itself. Think even how country folks, in many parts of England, in three months' time, may be crying out for rain, and afraid of short crops, and fever, and scarlatina, and cattle-plague, for want of the very water which we are now letting run back, wasted, into the sea from whence it came. And yet we call ourselves a civilised people."

It is not wise, I know, to preach to boys. And yet, sometimes, a man must speak his heart; even, like Midas's slave, to the reeds by the river side. And I had so often, fishing up and down full many a stream, whispered my story to those same river-reeds; and told them that my Lord the Sovereign Demos had, like old Midas, asses' ears in spite of all his gold, that I thought I might for once tell it the boy likewise, in hope that he might help his generation to mend that which my own generation does not seem like to mend.

I might have said more to him: but did not. For it is not well to destroy too early the child's illusion, that people must be wise because they are grown up, and have votes, and rule—or think they rule—the world. The child will find out how true that is soon enough for himself. If the truth be forced on him by the hot words of those with whom he lives, it is apt to breed in him that contempt, stormful and therefore barren, which makes revolutions; and not that pity, calm and therefore helpful, which makes reforms.

So I might have said to him, but did not—And then men pray for rain:

My boy, did you ever hear the old Eastern legend about the Gipsies? How they were such good musicians, that some great Indian Sultan sent for the whole tribe, and planted them near his palace, and gave them land, and ploughs to break it up, and seed to sow it, that they might dwell there, and play and sing to him.

But when the winter arrived, the Gipsies all came to the Sultan, and cried that they were starving. "But what have you done with the seed-corn which I gave you?" "O Light of the Age, we ate it in the summer." "And what have you done with the ploughs which I gave you?" "O Glory of the Universe, we burnt them to bake the corn withal."

Then said that great Sultan—"Like the butterflies you have lived; and like the butterflies you shall wander." So he drove them out. And that is how the Gipsies came hither from the East.

Now suppose that the Sultan of all Sultans, who sends the rain, should make a like answer to us foolish human beings, when we prayed for rain: "But what have you done with the rain which I gave you six months since?" "We have let it run into the sea." "Then, ere you ask for more rain, make places wherein you can keep it when you have it." "But that would be, in most cases, too expensive. We can employ our capital more profitably in other directions."

It is not for me to say what answer might be made to such an excuse. I think a child's still unsophisticated sense of right and wrong would soon supply one; and probably one—considering the complexity, and difficulty, and novelty, of the whole question—somewhat too harsh; as children's judgments are wont to be.

But would it not be well if our children, without being taught to blame anyone for what is past, were taught something about what ought to be done now, what must be done soon, with the rainfall of these islands; and about other and kindred health-questions, on the solution of which depends, and will depend more and more, the life of millions? One would have thought that those public schools and colleges which desire to monopolise the education of the owners of the soil; of the great employers of labour; of the clergy; and of all, indeed, who ought to be acquainted with the duties of property, the conditions of public health, and, in a word, with the general laws of what is now called Social Science—one would have thought, I say, that these public schools and colleges would have taught their scholars somewhat at least about such matters, that they might go forth into life with at least some rough notions of the causes which make people healthy or unhealthy, rich or poor, comfortable or wretched, useful or dangerous to the State. But as long as our great educational institutions, safe, or fancying themselves safe, in some enchanted castle, shut out by ancient magic from the living world, put a premium on Latin and Greek verses: a wise father will, during the holidays, talk now and then, I hope, somewhat after this fashion:

"You must understand, my boy, that all the water in the country comes out of the sky, and from nowhere else; and that, therefore, to save and store the water when it falls is a question of life and death to crops, and man, and beast; for with or without water is life or death. If I took, for instance, the water from the moors above and turned it over yonder field, I could double, and more than double, the crops in that field, henceforth."

"Then why do I not do it?"

"Only because the field lies higher than the house; and if—now here is one thing which you and every civilised man should know—if you have water-meadows, or any 'irrigated' land, as it is called, above a house, or, even on a level with it, it is certain to breed not merely cold and damp, but fever or ague. Our forefathers did not understand this; and they built their houses, as this is built, in the lowest places they could find: sometimes because they wanted to be near ponds, from whence they could get fish in Lent; but more often, I think, because they wanted to be sheltered from the wind. They had no glass, as we have, in their windows, or, at least, only latticed casements, which let in the wind and cold; and they shrank from high and exposed, and therefore really healthy, spots. But now that we have good glass, and sash windows, and doors that will shut tight, we can build warm houses where we like. And if you ever have to do with the building of cottages, remember that it is your duty

117

to the people who will live in them, and therefore to the State, to see that they stand high and dry, where no water can drain down into their foundations, and where fog, and the poisonous gases which are given out by rotting vegetables, cannot drain down either. You will learn more about all that when you learn, as every civilised lad should in these days, something about chemistry, and the laws of fluids and gases. But you know already that flowers are cut off by frost in the low grounds sooner than in the high; and that the fog at night always lies along the brooks; and that the sour moor-smell which warns us to shut our windows at sunset, comes down from the hill, and not up from the valley. Now all these things are caused by one and the same law; that cold air is heavier than warm; and, therefore, like so much water, must run down-hill."

"But what about the rainfall?"

"Well, I have wandered a little from the rainfall: though not as far as you fancy; for fever and ague and rheumatism usually mean—rain in the wrong place. But if you knew how much illness, and torturing pain, and death, and sorrow arise, even to this very day, from ignorance of these simple laws, then you would bear them carefully in mind, and wish to know more about them. But now for water being life to the beasts. Do you remember—though you are hardly old enough—the cattle-plague? How the beasts died, or had to be killed and buried, by tens of thousands; and how misery and ruin fell on hundreds of honest men and women over many of the richest counties of

England: but how we in this vale had no cattle-plague; and how there was none—as far as I recollect—in the uplands of Devon and Cornwall, nor of Wales, nor of the Scotch Highlands? Now, do you know why that was? Simply because we here, like those other up-landers, are in such a country as Palestine was before the foolish Jews cut down all their timber, and so destroyed their own rainfall—a 'land of brooks of water, of fountains and depths that spring out of valleys and hills.' There is hardly a field here that has not, thank God, its running brook, or its sweet spring, from which our cattle were drinking their health and life, while in the clay-lands of Cheshire, and in the Cambridgeshire fens—which were drained utterly dry—the poor things drank no water, too often, save that of the very same putrid ponds in which they had been standing all day long, to cool themselves, and to keep off the flies. I do not say, of course, that bad water caused the cattle-plague. It came by infection from the East of Europe. But I say that bad water made the cattle ready to take it, and made it spread over the country; and when you are old enough I will give you plenty of proof—some from the herds of your own kinsmen—that what I say is true."

"And as for pure water being life to human beings: why have we never fever here, and scarcely ever diseases like fever—zymotics, as the doctors call them? Or, if a case comes into our parish from outside, why does the fever never spread? For the very same reason that we had no cattle-plague. Because we have more pure water close to every cottage than we need. And this I tell you: that the only two outbreaks of deadly disease which we have had here for thirty years, were both of them, as far as I could see, to be traced to filthy water having got into the poor folks' wells. Water, you must remember, just as it is life when pure, is death when foul. For it can carry, unseen to the eye, and even when it looks clear and sparkling, and tastes soft and sweet, poisons which have perhaps killed more human beings than ever were killed in battle. You have read, perhaps, how the Athenians, when they were dying of the plague, accused the Lacedaemonians outside the walls of poisoning their wells; or how, in some of the pestilences of the Middle Ages, the common people used to accuse the poor harmless Jews of poisoning the wells, and set upon them and murdered them horribly. They were right, I do not doubt, in their notion that the well-water was giving them the pestilence: but they had not sense to see that they were poisoning the wells themselves by their dirt and carelessness; or, in the case of poor besieged Athens, probably by mere overcrowding, which has cost many a life ere now, and will cost more. And I am sorry to tell you, my little man, that even now too many people have no more sense than they had, and die in consequence. If you could see a battle-field, and men shot down, writhing and dying in hundreds by shell and bullet, would not that seem to you a horrid sight? Then—I do not wish to make you sad too early, but this is a fact that everyone should know—that more people, and not strong men only, but women and little children too, are killed and wounded in Great Britain every year by bad water and want of water together, than were killed and wounded in any battle which has been fought since you were born. Medical men know this well. And when you are older, you may see it for yourself in the Registrar-General's reports, blue-books, pamphlets, and so on, without end."

"But why do not people stop such a horrible loss of life?"

"Well, my dear boy, the true causes of it have only been known for the last thirty or forty years; and we English are, as good King Alfred found us to his sorrow a thousand years ago, very slow to move, even when we see a thing ought to be done. Let us hope that in this matter—we have been so in most matters as yet—we shall be like the tortoise in the fable, and not the hare; and by moving slowly, but surely, win the race at last."

"But now think for yourself: and see what you would do to save these people from being poisoned by bad water. Remember that the plain question is this: The rain-water comes down from heaven as water, and nothing but water. Rain-water is the only pure water, after all. How would you save that for the poor people who have none? There; run away and hunt rabbits on the moor: but look, meanwhile, how you would save some of this beautiful and precious water which is roaring away into the sea."

"Well? What would you do? Make ponds, you say, like the old monks' ponds, now all broken down. Dam all the glens across their mouths, and turn them into reservoirs."

"'Out of the mouths of babes and sucklings'—Well, that will have to be done. That is being done more and more, more or less well. The good people of Glasgow did it first, I think; and now the good people of Manchester, and of other northern towns, have done it, and have saved many a human life thereby already. But it must be done, some day, all over England and Wales, and great part of Scotland. For the mountain tops and moors, my boy, by a beautiful law of nature, compensate for their own poverty by yielding a wealth which the rich lowlands cannot yield. You do not understand? Then see. Yon moor above can grow neither corn nor grass. But one thing it can grow, and does grow, without which we should have no corn nor grass, and that is—water. Not only does far more rain fall up there than falls here down below, but even in drought the high moors condense the moisture into dew, and so yield some water, even when the lowlands are burnt up with drought. The reason of that you must learn hereafter. That it is so, you should know yourself. For on the high chalk downs, you know, where farmers make a sheep-pond, they never, if they are wise, make it in a valley or on a hillside, but on the bleakest top of the very highest down; and there, if they can once get it filled with snow and rain in winter, the blessed dews of night will keep some water in it all the summer through, while the ponds below are utterly dried up. And even so it is, as I know, with this very moor. Corn and grass it will not grow, because there is too little 'staple,' that is, soluble minerals, in the sandy soil. But how much water it might grow, you may judge roughly for yourself, by remembering how many brooks like this are running off it now to carry mere dirt into the river, and then into the sea."

"But why should we not make dams at once; and save the water?"

"Because we cannot afford it. No one would buy the water when we had stored it. The rich in town and country will always take care—and quite right they are—to have water enough for themselves, and for their servants too, whatever it may cost them. But the poorer people are—and therefore usually, alas! the more ignorant—the less water they get; and the less they care to have water; and the less they are inclined to pay for it; and the more, I am sorry to say, they waste what little they do get; and I am still more sorry to say, spoil, and even steal and sell—in London at least—the stop-cocks and lead-pipes which bring the water into their houses. So that keeping a water-shop is a very troublesome and uncertain business; and one which is not likely to pay us or anyone round here."

"But why not let some company manage it, as they manage railways, and gas, and other things?"

"Ah—you have been overhearing a good deal about companies of late, I see. But this I will tell you; that when you grow up, and have a vote and influence, it will be your duty, if you intend to be a good citizen, not only not to put the water-supply of England into the hands of fresh companies, but to help to take out of their hands what water-supply they manage already, especially in London; and likewise the gas-supply; and the railroads; and everything else, in a word, which everybody uses, and must use. For you must understand—at least as soon as you can—that though the men who make up companies are no worse than other men, and some of them, as you ought to know, very good men; yet what they have to look to is their profits; and the less water they supply, and the worse it is, the more profit they make. For most water, I am sorry to say, is fouled before the water companies can get to it, as this water which runs past us will be, and as the Thames water above London is. Therefore it has to be cleansed, or partly cleansed, at a very great expense. So water companies have to be inspected— in plain English, watched—at a very heavy expense to the nation by Government officers; and compelled to do their best, and take their utmost care. And so it has come to pass that the London water is not now nearly as bad as some of it was thirty years ago, when it was no more fit to drink than that in the cattle-yard tank. But still we must have more water, and better, in London; for it is growing year by year. There are more than three millions of people already in what we call London; and ere you are an old man there may be between four and five millions. Now to supply all these people with water is a duty which we must not leave to any private companies. It must be done by a public authority, as is fit and proper in a free self-governing country. In this matter, as in all others, we will try to do what the Royal Commission told us four years ago we ought to do. I hope that you will see, though I may not, the day when what we call London, but which is really nine-tenths of it, only a great nest of separate villages huddled together, will be divided into three great self-governing cities, London, Westminster, and Southwark; each with its own corporation, like that of the venerable and well-governed city of London; each managing its own water-supply, gas-supply, and sewage, and other matters besides; and managing them, like Dublin, Glasgow, Manchester, Liverpool, and other great northern towns, far more cheaply and far better than any companies can do it for them."

"But where shall we get water enough for all these millions of people? There are no mountains near London. But we might give them the water off our moors."

"No, no, my boy,

"He that will not when he may,
When he will, he shall have nay."

Some fifteen years ago the Londoners might have had water from us; and I was one of those who did my best to get it for them: but the water companies did not choose to take it; and now this part of England is growing so populous and so valuable that it wants all its little rainfall for itself. So there is another leaf torn out of the Sibylline books for the poor old water companies. You do not understand: you will some day. But you may comfort yourself about London. For it happens to be, I think, the luckiest city in the world; and if it had not been, we should have had pestilence on pestilence in it, as terrible as the great plague of Charles II.'s time. The old Britons, without knowing in the least what they were doing, settled old London city in the very centre of the most wonderful natural reservoir in this island, or perhaps in all Europe; which reaches from Kent into Wiltshire, and round again into Suffolk; and that is, the dear old chalk downs."

"Why, they are always dry."

"Yes. But the turf on them never burns up, and the streams which flow through them never run dry, and seldom or never flood either. Do you not know, from Winchester, that that is true? Then where is all the rain and snow gone, which falls on them year by year, but into the chalk itself, and into the green-sands, too, below the chalk? There it is, soaked up as by a sponge, in quantity incalculable; enough, some think, to supply London, let it grow as huge as it may. I wish I too were sure of that. But the Commission has shown itself so wise and fair, and brave likewise—too brave, I am sorry to say, for some who might have supported them—that it is not for me to gainsay their opinion."

"But if there was not water enough in the chalk, are not the Londoners rich enough to bring it from any distance?"

"My boy, in this also we will agree with the Commission—that we ought not to rob Peter to pay Paul, and take water to a distance which other people close at hand may want. Look at the map of England and southern Scotland; and see for yourself what is just, according to geography and nature. There are four mountain-ranges; four great water-fields. First, the hills of the Border. Their rainfall ought to be stored for the Lothians and the extreme north of England. Then the Yorkshire and Derbyshire Hills—the central chine of England. Their rainfall is being stored already, to the honour of the shrewd northern men, for the manufacturing counties east and west of the hills. Then come the Lake mountains—the finest water-field of all, because more rain by far falls there than in any place in England. But they will be wanted to supply Lancashire, and some day Liverpool itself; for Liverpool is now using rain which belongs more justly to other towns; and besides, there are plenty of counties and towns, down into Cheshire, which would be glad of what water Lancashire does not want. At last come the Snowdon mountains, a noble water-field, which I know well; for an old dream of mine has been, that ere I died I should see all the rain of the Carnedds, and the Glyders, and Siabod, and Snowdon itself, carried across the Conway river to feed the mining districts of North Wales, where the streams are now all foul with oil and lead; and then on into the western coal and iron fields, to Wolverhampton and Birmingham itself: and if I were the engineer who got that done, I should be happier—prouder I dare not say—than if I had painted nobler pictures than Raffaelle, or written nobler plays than Shakespeare. I say that, boy, in most deliberate earnest. But meanwhile, do you not see that in districts where coal and iron may be found, and fresh manufactures may spring up any day in any place, each district has a right to claim the nearest rainfall for itself? And now, when we have got the water into its proper place, let us see what we shall do with it."

"But why do you say 'we'? Can you and I do all this?"

"My boy, are not you and I free citizens; part of the people, the Commons—as the good old word runs—of this country? And are we not—or ought we not to be in time—beside that, educated men? By the people, remember, I mean, not only the hand-working man who has just got a vote; I mean the clergy of all denominations; and the gentlemen of the press; and last, but not least, the scientific men. If those four classes together were to tell every government—'Free water we will have, and as much as we reasonably choose;' and tell every candidate for the House of Commons: 'Unless you promise to get us as much free water as we reasonably choose, we will not return you to Parliament:' then, I think, we four should put such a 'pressure' on Government as no water companies, or other vested interests, could long resist. And if any of those four classes should hang back, and waste their time and influence over matters far less important and less pressing, the other three must laugh at them, and more than laugh at them; and ask them: 'Why have you education, why have you influence, why have you votes, why are you freemen and not slaves, if not to preserve the comfort, the decency, the health, the lives of men, women, and children—most of those latter your own wives and your own children?'"

"But what shall we do with the water?"

"Well, after all, that is a more practical matter than speculations grounded on the supposition that all classes will do their duty. But the first thing we will do will be to give to the very poorest houses a constant supply, at high pressure; so that everybody may take as much water as he likes, instead of having to keep the water in little cisterns, where it gets foul and putrid only too often."

"But will they not waste it then?"

"So far from it, wherever the water has been laid on at high pressure, the waste, which is terrible now— some say that in London one-third of the water is wasted—begins to lessen; and both water and expense are saved. If you will only think, you will see one reason why. If a woman leaves a high-pressure tap running, she will flood her place and her neighbour's too. She will be like the magician's servant, who called up the demon to draw water for him; and so he did: but when he had begun he would not stop, and if the magician had not come home, man and house would have been washed away."

"But if it saves money, why do not the water companies do it?"

"Because—and really here there are many excuses for the poor old water companies, when so many

of them swerve and gib at the very mention of constant water-supply, like a poor horse set to draw a load
which he feels is too heavy for him—because, to keep
everything in order among dirty, careless, and often
drunken people, there must be officers with lawful
authority—water-policemen we will call them—who
can enter people's houses when they will, and if they
find anything wrong with the water, set it to rights
with a high hand, and even summon the people who
have set it wrong. And that is a power which, in a free
country, must never be given to the servants of any
private company, but only to the officers of a corporation or of the Government."

"And what shall we do with the rest of the water?"

"Well, we shall have, I believe, so much to spare
that we may at least do this: In each district of each
city, and the centre of each town, we may build
public baths and lavatories, where poor men and
women may get their warm baths when they will;
for now they usually never bathe at all, because they
will not—and ought not, if they be hard-worked
folk—bathe in cold water during nine months of the
year. And there they shall wash their clothes, and
dry them by steam; instead of washing them as now,
at home, either under back sheds, where they catch
cold and rheumatism, or too often, alas! in their own
living rooms, in an atmosphere of foul vapour, which
drives the father to the public-house and the children into the streets; and which not only prevents
the clothes from being thoroughly dried again, but

is, my dear boy, as you will know when you are older, a very hot-bed of disease. And they shall have other comforts, and even luxuries, these public lavatories; and be made, in time, graceful and refining, as well as merely useful. Nay, we will even, I think, have in front of each of them a real fountain; not like the drinking-fountains—though they are great and needful boons—which you see here and there about the streets, with a tiny dribble of water to a great deal of expensive stone: but real fountains, which shall leap, and sparkle, and plash, and gurgle; and fill the place with life, and light, and coolness; and sing in the people's ears the sweetest of all earthly songs—save the song of a mother over her child—the song of 'The Laughing Water.'"

"But will not that be a waste?"

"Yes, my boy. And for that very reason, I think we, the people, will have our fountains; if it be but to make our governments, and corporations, and all public bodies and officers, remember that they all—save Her Majesty the Queen—are our servants, and not we theirs; and that we choose to have water, not only to wash with, but to play with, if we like. And I believe—for the world, as you will find, is full not only of just but of generous souls—that if the water-supply were set really right, there would be found, in many a city, many a generous man who, over and above his compulsory water-rate, would give his poor fellow-townsmen such a real fountain as those which ennoble the great square at Carcasonne and the great square at Nismes; to be 'a thing of beauty and a joy for ever.'"

"And now, if you want to go back to your Latin and Greek, you shall translate for me into Latin—I do not expect you to do it into Greek, though it would turn very well into Greek, for the Greeks know all about the matter long before the Romans—what follows here; and you shall verify the facts and the names, etc., in it from your dictionaries of antiquity and biography, that you may remember all the better what it says. And by that time, I think, you will have learnt something more useful to yourself, and, I hope, to your country hereafter, than if you had learnt to patch together the neatest Greek and Latin verses which have appeared since the days of Mr. Canning."

I have often amused myself, by fancying one question which an old Roman emperor would ask, were he to rise from his grave and visit the sights of London under the guidance of some minister of state. The august shade would, doubtless, admire our railroads and bridges, our cathedrals and our public parks, and much more of which we need not be ashamed. But after awhile, I think, he would look round, whether in London or in most of our great cities, inquiringly and in vain, for one class of buildings, which in his empire were wont to be almost as conspicuous and as splendid, because, in public opinion, almost as necessary, as the basilicas and temples: "And where," he would ask, "are your public baths?" And if the minister of state who was his guide should answer: "Oh great Caesar, I really do not know. I believe there are some somewhere at the back of that ugly building which we call the National Gallery; and I think there have been some meetings lately in the East End, and an amateur concert at the Albert Hall, for restoring, by private subscriptions, some baths and wash-houses in Bethnal Green, which had fallen to decay. And there may be two or three more about the metropolis; for parish vestries have powers by Act of Parliament to establish such places, if they think fit, and choose to pay for them out of the rates." Then, I think, the august shade might well make answer: "We used to call you, in old Rome, northern barbarians. It seems that you have not lost all your barbarian habits. Are you aware that, in every city in the Roman empire, there were, as a matter of course, public baths open, not only to the poorest freeman, but to the slave, usually for the payment of the smallest current coin, and often gratuitously? Are you aware that in Rome itself, millionaire after millionaire, emperor after emperor, from Menenius Agrippa and Nero down to Diocletian and Constantine, built baths, and yet more baths; and connected with them gymnasia for exercise, lecture-rooms, libraries, and porticoes, wherein the people might have shade, and shelter, and rest? I remark, by-the-bye, that I have not seen in all your London a single covered place in which the people may take shelter during a shower. Are you aware that these baths were of the most magnificent architecture, decorated with marbles, paintings, sculptures, fountains, what not? And yet I had heard, in Hades down below, that you prided yourselves here on the study of the learned languages; and, indeed, taught little but Greek and Latin at your public schools?"

Then, if the minister should make reply: "Oh yes, we know all this. Even since the revival of letters in the end of the fifteenth century a whole literature has been written—a great deal of it, I fear, by pedants who seldom washed even their hands and faces—about your Greek and Roman baths. We visit their colossal ruins in Italy and elsewhere with awe and admiration; and the discovery of a new Roman bath in any old city of our isles sets all our antiquaries buzzing with interest."

"Then why," the shade might ask, "do you not copy an example which you so much admire? Surely England must be much in want, either of water, or of fuel to heat it with?"

"On the contrary, our rainfall is almost too great; our soil so damp that we have had to invent a whole art of subsoil drainage unknown to you; while, as for fuel, our coal-mines make us the great fuel-exporting people of the world."

What a quiet sneer might curl the lip of a Constantine as he replied: "Not in vain, as I said, did we call you, some fifteen hundred years ago, the barbarians of the north. But tell me, good barbarian, whom I know to be both brave and wise—for the fame of your young British empire has reached us even in the realms below, and we recognise in you, with all respect, a people more like us Romans than any which has appeared on earth for many centuries—how is it you have forgotten that sacred duty of keeping the people clean, which you surely at one time learnt from us? When your ancestors entered our armies, and rose, some of them, to be great generals, and even emperors, like those two Teuton peasants, Justin and Justinian, who, long after my days, reigned in my own Constantinople: then, at least, you saw baths, and used them; and felt, after the bath, that you were civilised men, and not 'sordidi ac foetentes,' as we used to call you when fresh out of your bullock-waggons and cattle-pens. How is it that you have forgotten that lesson?"

The minister, I fear, would have to answer that our ancestors were barbarous enough, not only to destroy the Roman cities, and temples, and basilicas, and statues, but the Roman baths likewise; and then retired, each man to his own freehold in the country, to live a life not much more cleanly or more graceful than that of the swine which were his favourite food. But he would have a right to plead, as an excuse, that not only in England, but throughout the whole of the conquered Latin empire, the Latin priesthood, who, in some respects, were—to their honour—the representatives of Roman civilisation and the protectors of its remnants, were the determined enemies of its cleanliness; that they looked on personal dirt—like the old hermits of the Thebaid—as a sign of sanctity; and discouraged—as they are said to do still in some of the Romance countries of Europe—the use of the bath, as not only luxurious, but also indecent.

At which answer, it seems to me, another sneer might curl the lip of the august shade, as he said to himself: "This, at least, I did not expect, when I made Christianity the state religion of my empire. But you, good barbarian, look clean enough. You do not look on dirt as a sign of sanctity?"

"On the contrary, sire, the upper classes of our empire boast of being the cleanliest—perhaps the only perfectly cleanly—people in the world: except, of course, the savages of the South Seas. And dirt is so far from being a thing which we admire, that our scientific men—than whom the world has never seen wiser—have proved to us, for a whole generation past, that dirt is the fertile cause of disease and drunkenness, misery, and recklessness."

"And, therefore," replies the shade, ere he disappears, "of discontent and revolution: followed by a tyranny endured, as in Rome and many another place, by men once free; because tyranny will at least do for them what they are too lazy, and cowardly, and greedy, to do for themselves. Farewell, and prosper; as you seem likely to prosper, on the whole. But if you wish me to consider you a civilised nation: let me hear that you have brought a great river from the depths of the earth, be they a thousand fathoms deep, or from your nearest mountains, be they five hundred miles away; and have washed out London's dirt—and your own shame. Till then, abstain from judging too harshly a Constantine, or even a Caracalla; for they, whatever were their sins, built baths, and kept their people clean. But do your gymnasia—your schools and universities, teach your youth naught about all this?"

THE TREE OF KNOWLEDGE

The more I have contemplated that ancient story of the Fall, the more it has seemed to me within the range of probability, and even of experience. It must have happened somewhere for the first time; for it has happened only too many times since. It has happened, as far as I can ascertain, in every race, and every age, and every grade of civilisation. It is happening round us now in every region of the globe. Always and everywhere, it seems to me, have poor human beings been tempted to eat of some "tree of knowledge," that they may be, even for an hour, as gods; wise, but with a false wisdom; careless, but with a frantic carelessness; and happy, but with a happiness which, when the excitement is past, leaves too often—as with that hapless pair in Eden—depression, shame, and fear. Everywhere, and in all ages, as far as I can ascertain, has man been inventing stimulants and narcotics to supply that want of vitality of which he is so painfully aware; and has asked nature, and not God, to clear the dull brain, and comfort the weary spirit.

This has been, and will be perhaps for many a century to come, almost the most fearful failing of this poor, exceptional, over-organised, diseased, and truly fallen being called Man, who is in doubt daily whether he be a god or an ape; and in trying wildly to become the former, ends but too often in becoming the latter.

For man, whether savage or civilised, feels, and has felt in every age, that there is something wrong with him. He usually confesses this fact—as is to be expected—of his fellow-men, rather than of himself; and shows his sense that there is something wrong with them by complaining of, hating, and killing them. But he cannot always conceal from himself the fact that he, too, is wrong, as well as they; and as he will not usually kill himself, he tries wild ways to make himself at least feel—if not to be—somewhat "better." Philosophers may bid him be content; and tell him that he is what he ought to be, and what nature has made him. But he cares nothing for the philosophers. He knows, usually, that he is not what he ought to be; that he carries about with him, in most cases, a body more or less diseased and decrepit, incapable of doing all the work which he feels that he himself could do, or expressing all the emotions which he himself longs to express; a dull brain and dull senses, which cramp the eager infinity within him; as—so Goethe once said with pity—the horse's single hoof cramps the fine intelligence and generosity of his nature, and forbids him even to grasp an object, like the more stupid cat, and baser monkey. And man has a self, too, within, from which he longs too often to escape, as from a household ghost; who pulls out, at unfortunately rude and unwelcome hours, the ledger of memory. And so when the tempter—be he who he may—says to him, "Take this, and you will 'feel better.' Take this, and you shall be as gods, knowing good and evil:" then, if the temptation was, as the old story says, too much for man while healthy and unfallen, what must it be for his unhealthy and fallen children?

In vain we say to man:

> 'Tis life, not death, for which you pant;
> 'Tis life, whereof your nerves are scant;
> More life, and fuller, that you want.

And your tree of knowledge is not the tree of life: it is in every case, the tree of death; of decrepitude, madness, misery. He prefers the voice of the tempter: "Thou shalt not surely die." Nay, he will say at last: "Better be as gods awhile, and die: than be the crawling, insufficient thing I am; and live."

He—did I say? Alas! I must say she likewise. The sacred story is only too true to fact, when it represents the woman as falling, not merely at the same time as the man, but before the man. Only let us remember that it represents the woman as tempted; tempted, seemingly, by a rational being, of lower race, and yet of superior cunning; who must, therefore, have fallen before the woman. Who or what the being was, who is called the Serpent in our translation of Genesis, it is not for me to say. We have absolutely, I think, no facts from which to judge; and Rabbinical traditions need trouble no man much. But I fancy that a missionary, preaching on this story to Negroes; telling them plainly that the "Serpent" meant the first Obeah man; and then comparing the experiences of that hapless pair in Eden, with their own after certain orgies not yet extinct in Africa and elsewhere, would be only too well understood: so well, indeed, that he might run some risk of eating himself, not of the tree of life, but of that of death. The sorcerer or sorceress tempting the woman; and then the woman tempting the man; this seems to be, certainly among savage peoples, and, alas! too often among civilised peoples also, the usual course of the world-wide tragedy.

But—paradoxical as it may seem—the woman's yielding before the man is not altogether to her dishonour, as those old monks used to allege who hated, and too often tortured, the sex whom they could not enjoy. It is not to the woman's dishonour, if she felt, before her husband, higher aspirations than those after mere animal pleasure. To be as gods, knowing good and evil, is a vain and foolish, but not a base and brutal, wish. She proved herself thereby—though at an awful cost— a woman, and not an animal. And indeed the woman's more delicate organisation, her more vivid emotions, her more voluble fancy, as well as her mere physical weakness and weariness, have been to her, in all ages, a special source of temptation; which it is to her honour that she has resisted so much better than the physically stronger, and therefore more culpable, man.

As for what the tree of knowledge was, there really is no need for us to waste our time in guessing. If it was not one plant, then it was another. It may have been something which has long since perished off the earth. It may have been—as some learned men have guessed—the sacred Soma, or Homa, of the early Brahmin race; and that may have been a still existing narcotic species of Asclepias. It certainly was not the vine. The language of the Hebrew Scripture concerning it, and the sacred use to which it is consecrated in the Gospels, forbid that notion utterly; at least to those who know enough of antiquity to pass by, with a smile, the theory that the wines mentioned in Scripture were not intoxicating. And yet—as a fresh corroboration of what I am trying to say—how fearfully has that noble gift to man been abused for the same end as a hundred other vegetable products, ever since those mythic days when Dionusos brought the vine from the far East, amid troops of human Maenads and half-human Satyrs; and the Bacchae tore Pentheus in pieces on Cithaeron, for daring to intrude upon their sacred rites; and since those historic days, too, when, less than two hundred years before the Christian era, the Bacchic rites spread from Southern Italy into Etruria, and thence to the matrons of Rome; and under the guidance of Poenia Annia, a Campanian lady, took at last shapes of which no man must speak, but which had to be put down with terrible but just severity, by the Consuls and the Senate.

But it matters little, I say, what this same tree of knowledge was. Was every vine on earth destroyed to-morrow, and every vegetable also from which alcohol is now distilled, man would soon discover something else wherewith to satisfy the insatiate craving. Has he not done so already? Has not almost every people had its tree of knowledge, often more deadly than any distilled liquor, from the absinthe of the cultivated Frenchman, and the opium of the cultivated Chinese, down to the bush-poisons wherewith the tropic sorcerer initiates his dupes into the knowledge of good and evil, and the fungus from which the Samoiede extracts in autumn a few days of brutal happiness, before the setting in of the long six months' night? God grant that modern science may not bring to light fresh substitutes for alcohol, opium, and the rest; and give the white races, in that state of effeminate and godless quasi-civilisation which I sometimes fear is creeping upon them, fresh means of destroying themselves delicately and pleasantly off the face of the earth.

It is said by some that drunkenness is on the increase in this island. I have no trusty proof of it: but I can believe it possible; for every cause of drunkenness seems on the increase. Overwork of body and mind; circumstances which depress health; temptation to drink, and drink again, at every corner of the streets; and finally, money, and ever more money, in the hands of uneducated people, who have not the desire, and too often not the means, of spending it in any save the lowest pleasures. These, it seems to me, are the true causes of drunkenness, increasing or not. And if we wish to become a more temperate nation, we must lessen them, if we cannot eradicate them.

First, overwork. We all live too fast, and work too hard. "All things are full of labour, man cannot utter it." In the heavy struggle for existence which goes on all around us, each man is tasked more and more—if he be really worth buying and using—to the utmost of his powers all day long. The weak have to compete on equal terms with the strong; and crave, in consequence, for artificial strength. How we shall stop that I know not, while every man is "making haste to be rich, and piercing himself through with many sorrows, and falling into foolish and hurtful lusts, which drown men in destruction and perdition." How we shall stop that, I say, I know not. The old prophet may have been right when he said: "Surely it is not of the Lord that the people shall labour in the very fire, and weary themselves for very vanity;" and in some juster, wiser, more sober system of society—somewhat more like the Kingdom of The Father come on earth—it may be that poor human beings will not need to toil so hard, and to keep themselves up to their work by stimulants, but will have time to sit down, and look around them, and think of God, and God's quiet universe, with something of quiet in themselves; something of rational leisure, and manful sobriety of mind, as well as of body.

But it seems to me also, that in such a state of society, when—as it was once well put—"every one has stopped running about like rats:"—that those who work hard, whether with muscle or with brain, would not be surrounded, as now, with every circumstance which tempts toward drink; by every circumstance which depresses the vital energies, and leaves them an easy prey to pestilence itself; by bad light, bad air, bad food, bad water, bad smells, bad occupations, which weaken the muscles, cramp the chest, disorder the digestion. Let any rational man, fresh from the country—in which I presume God, having made it, meant all men, more or less, to live—go through the back streets of any city, or through whole districts of the "black countries" of England; and then ask himself: Is it the will of God that His human children should live and toil in such dens, such deserts, such dark places of the earth? Lot him ask himself: Can they live and toil there without contracting a probably diseased habit of body; without contracting a certainly dull, weary, sordid habit of mind, which craves for any pleasure, however brutal, to escape from its own stupidity and emptiness? When I run through, by rail, certain parts of the iron-producing country— streets of furnaces, collieries, slag heaps, mud, slop, brick house-rows, smoke, dirt—and that is all; and when I am told, whether truly or falsely, that the main thing which the well-paid and well-fed men of those abominable wastes care for is—good fighting-dogs: I can only answer, that I am not surprised.

I say—as I have said elsewhere, and shall do my best to say it again—that the craving for drink and narcotics, especially that engendered in our great cities, is not a disease, but a symptom of disease; of a far deeper disease than any which drunkenness can produce; namely, of the growing degeneracy of a population striving in vain by stimulants and narcotics to fight against those slow poisons with which our greedy barbarism, miscalled civilisation, has surrounded them from the cradle to the grave. I may be answered that the old German, Angle, Dane, drank heavily. I know it: but why did they drink, save for the same reason that the fenman drank, and his wife took opium, at least till the fens were drained? why but to keep off the depressing effects of the malaria of swamps and new clearings, which told on them—who always settled in the lowest grounds—in the shape of fever and ague? Here it may be answered again that stimulants have been, during the memory of man, the destruction of the Red Indian race in America. I reply boldly that I do not believe it. There is evidence enough in Jacques Cartier's "Voyages to the Rivers of Canada;" and evidence more than enough in Strachey's "Travaile in Virginia"—to quote only two authorities out of many—to prove that the Red Indians, when the white man first met with them, were, in North and South alike, a diseased, decaying, and, as all their traditions confess, decreasing race. Such a race would naturally crave for "the water of life," the "usquebagh," or whisky, as we have contracted the old name now. But I should have thought that the white man, by introducing among these poor creatures iron, fire-arms, blankets, and above all, horses wherewith to follow the buffalo-herds, which they could never follow on foot, must have done ten times more towards keeping them alive, than he has done towards destroying them by giving them the chance of a week's drunkenness twice a year, when they came in to his forts to sell the skins which, without his gifts, they would never have got.

Such a race would, of course, if wanting vitality, crave for stimulants. But if the stimulants, and not the original want of vitality, combined with morals utterly detestable, and worthy only of the gallows—and here I know what I say, and dare not tell what I know, from eye-witnesses—have been the cause of the Red Indians' extinction, then how is it, let me ask, that the Irishman and the Scotsman have, often to their great harm, been drinking as much whisky—and usually very bad whisky—not merely twice a year, but as often as they could get it, during the whole Iron Age, and, for aught anyone can tell, during the Bronze Age, and the Stone Age before that, and yet are still the most healthy, able, valiant, and prolific races in Europe? Had they drunk less whisky they would, doubtless, have been more healthy, able, valiant, and perhaps even *more* prolific, than they are now. They show no sign, however, as yet, of going the way of the Red Indian.

But if the craving for stimulants and narcotics is a token of deficient vitality, then the deadliest foe of that craving, and all its miserable results, is surely the

Sanatory Reformer; the man who preaches, and—as far as ignorance and vested interests will allow him, procures—for the masses, pure air, pure sunlight, pure water, pure dwelling-houses, pure food. Not merely every fresh drinking-fountain, but every fresh public bath and wash-house, every fresh open space, every fresh growing tree, every fresh open window, every fresh flower in that window—each of these is so much, as the old Persians would have said, conquered for Ormuzd, the god of light and life, out of the dominion of Ahriman, the king of darkness and of death; so much taken from the causes of drunkenness and disease, and added to the causes of sobriety and health.

Meanwhile one thing is clear: that if this present barbarism and anarchy of covetousness, miscalled modern civilisation, were tamed and drilled into something more like a Kingdom of God on earth, then we should not see the reckless and needless multiplication of liquor shops, which disgraces this country now.

As a single instance: in one country parish of nine hundred inhabitants, in which the population has increased only one-ninth in the last fifty years, there are now practically eight public-houses, where fifty years ago there were but two. One, that is, for every hundred and ten—or rather, omitting children, farmers, shop-keepers, gentlemen, and their households, one for every fifty of the inhabitants. In the face of the allurements, often of the basest kind, which these dens offer, the clergyman and the schoolmaster struggle in vain to keep up night schools and young men's clubs, and to inculcate habits of providence.

The young labourers over a great part of the south and east, at least of England—though never so well off, for several generations, as they are now—are growing up thriftless, shiftless; inferior, it seems to me, to their grandfathers in everything, save that they can usually read and write, and their grandfathers could not; and that they wear smart cheap cloth clothes, instead of their grandfathers' smock-frocks.

And if it be so in the country, how must it be in towns? There must come a thorough change in the present licensing system, in spite of all the "pressure" which certain powerful vested interests may bring to bear on governments. And it is the duty of every good citizen, who cares for his countrymen, and for their children after them, to help in bringing about that change as speedily as possible.

Again: I said just now that a probable cause of increasing drunkenness was the increasing material prosperity of thousands who knew no recreation beyond low animal pleasure. If I am right—and I believe that I am right—I must urge on those who wish drunkenness to decrease, the necessity of providing more, and more refined, recreation for the people.

Men drink, and women too, remember, not merely to supply exhaustion, not merely to drive away care; but often simply to drive away dulness. They have nothing to do save to think over what they have done in the day, or what they expect to do to-morrow; and they escape from that dreary round of business thought in liquor or narcotics. There are still those, by no means of the hand-working class, but absorbed all day by business, who drink heavily at night in their own comfortable homes, simply to recreate their over-burdened minds. Such cases, doubtless, are far less common than they were fifty years ago: but why? Is not the decrease of drinking among the richer classes certainly due to the increased refinement and variety of their tastes and occupations? In cultivating the aesthetic side of man's nature; in engaging him with the beautiful, the pure, the wonderful, the truly natural; with painting, poetry, music, horticulture, physical science—in all this lies recreation, in the true and literal sense of that word, namely, the re-creating and mending of the exhausted mind and feelings, such as no rational man will now neglect, either for himself, his children, or his workpeople.

But how little of all this is open to the masses, all should know but too well. How little opportunity the average hand-worker, or his wife, has of eating of any tree of knowledge, save of the very basest kind, is but too palpable. We are mending, thank God, in this respect. Free libraries and museums have sprung up of late in other cities beside London. God's blessing rest upon them all. And the Crystal Palace, and still later, the Bethnal Green Museum, have been, I believe, of far more use than many average sermons and lectures from many average orators.

But are we not still far behind the old Greeks, and the Romans of the Empire likewise, in the amount of amusement and instruction, and even of shelter, which we provide for the people? Recollect the—to me—disgraceful fact, that there is not, as far as I am aware, throughout the whole of London, a single portico or other covered place, in which the people can take refuge during a shower: and this in the climate of England! Where they do take refuge on a wet day the publican knows but too well; as he knows also where thousands of the lower classes, simply for want of any other place to be in, save their own sordid dwellings, spend as much as they are permitted of the Sabbath day. Let us put down "Sunday drinking" by all means, if we can. But let us remember that by closing the public-houses on Sunday, we prevent no man or woman from carrying home as much poison as they choose on Saturday night, to brutalise themselves therewith, perhaps for eight-and-forty hours. And let us see—in the name of Him who said that He had made the Sabbath for man, and not man for the Sabbath—let us see, I say, if we cannot do something to prevent the townsman's Sabbath being, not a day of rest, but a day of mere idleness; the day of most temptation, because of most dulness, of the whole seven.

And here, perhaps some sweet soul may look up reprovingly and say: "He talks of rest. Does he forget, and would he have the working man forget, that all these outward palliatives will never touch the seat of the disease, the unrest of the soul within? Does he forget, and would he have the working man forget, who it was who said—who only has the right to say: "Come unto Me, all ye who are weary and heavy laden, and I will give you rest"? Ah no, sweet soul. I know your words are true. I know that what we all want is inward rest; rest of heart and brain; the calm, strong, self-contained, self-denying character; which needs no stimulants, for it has no fits of depression; which needs no narcotics, for it has no fits of excitement; which needs no ascetic restraints, for it is strong enough to use God's gifts without abusing them; the character, in a word, which is truly temperate, not in drink or food merely, but in all desires, thoughts, and actions; freed from the wild lusts and ambitions to which that old Adam yielded, and, seeking for light and life by means forbidden, found thereby disease and death. Yes, I know that; and know, too, that that rest is found only where you have already found it.

And yet, in such a world as this, governed by a Being who has made sunshine, and flowers, and green grass, and the song of birds, and happy human smiles, and who would educate by them—if we would let Him—His human children from the cradle to the grave; in such a world as this, will you grudge any particle of that education, even any harmless substitute for it, to those spirits in prison whose surroundings too often tempt them, from the cradle to the grave, to fancy that the world is composed of bricks and iron, and governed by inspectors and policemen? Preach to those spirits in prison, as you know far better than we parsons how to preach; but let them have besides some glimpses of the splendid fact, that outside their prison-house is a world which God, not man, has made; wherein grows everywhere that tree of knowledge, which is likewise the tree of life; and that they have a right to some small share of its beauty, and its wonder, and its rest, for their own health of soul and body, and for the health of their children after them.

GREAT CITIES AND THEIR INFLUENCE
FOR GOOD AND EVIL [9]

The pleasure, gentlemen and ladies, of addressing you here is mixed in my mind with very solemn feelings; the honour which you have done me is tempered by humiliating thoughts.

For it was in this very city of Bristol, twenty-seven years ago, that I received my first lesson in what is now called Social Science; and yet, alas! more than ten years elapsed ere I could even spell out that lesson, though it had been written for me (as well as for all England) in letters of flame, from the one end of heaven to the other.

I was a school-boy in Clifton up above. I had been hearing of political disturbances, even of riots, of which I understood nothing, and for which I cared nothing. But on one memorable Sunday afternoon I saw an object which was distinctly not political. Otherwise I should have no right to speak of it here.

---

9   Lecture delivered at Bristol, October 5, 1857.

It was an afternoon of sullen autumn rain. The fog hung thick over the docks and lowlands. Glaring through that fog I saw a bright mass of flame—almost like a half-risen sun.

That, I was told, was the gate of the new gaol on fire. That the prisoners in it had been set free; that— But why speak of what too many here recollect but too well? The fog rolled slowly upward. Dark figures, even at that great distance, were flitting to and fro across what seemed the mouth of the pit. The flame increased—multiplied—at one point after another; till by ten o'clock that night I seemed to be looking down upon Dante's Inferno, and to hear the multitudinous moan and wail of the lost spirits surging to and fro amid that sea of fire.

Right behind Brandon Hill—how can I ever forget it?—rose the great central mass of fire; till the little mound seemed converted into a volcano, from the peak of which the flame streamed up, not red alone, but, delicately green and blue, pale rose and pearly white, while crimson sparks leapt and fell again in the midst of that rainbow, not of hope, but of despair; and dull explosions down below mingled with the roar of the mob, and the infernal hiss and crackle of the flame.

Higher and higher the fog was scorched and shrivelled upward by the fierce heat below, glowing through and through with red reflected glare, till it arched itself into one vast dome of red-hot iron, fit roof for all the madness down below—and beneath it, miles away, I could see the lonely tower of Dundie

shining red;—the symbol of the old faith, looking
down in stately wonder and sorrow upon the fearful
birth-throes of a new age. Yes.—Why did I say just
now despair? I was wrong. Birth-throes, and not death
pangs, those horrors were. Else they would have no
place in my discourse; no place, indeed, in my mind.
Why talk over the signs of disease, decay, death? Let
the dead bury their dead, and let us follow Him who
dieth not; by whose command

> *The old order changeth, giving place to the new,*
> *And God fulfils himself in many ways.*

If we will believe this,—if we will look on each
convulsion of society, however terrible for the time
being, as a token, not of decrepitude, but of youth;
not as the expiring convulsions of sinking humanity,
but as upward struggles, upward toward fuller light,
freer air, a juster, simpler, and more active life;—then
we shall be able to look calmly, however sadly, on the
most appalling tragedies of humanity—even on these
late Indian ones—and take our share, faithful and
hopeful, in supplying the new and deeper wants of a
new and nobler time.

But to return. It was on the Tuesday or Wednes-
day after, if I recollect right, that I saw another,
and a still more awful sight. Along the north side
of Queen Square, in front of ruins which had been
three days before noble buildings, lay a ghastly row,
not of corpses, but of corpse-fragments. I have no
more wish than you to dilate upon that sight. But

there was one charred fragment—with a scrap of old red petticoat adhering to it, which I never forgot—which I trust in God that I never shall forget. It is good for a man to be brought once at least in his life face to face with fact, ultimate fact, however horrible it may be; and have to confess to himself, shuddering, what things are possible upon God's earth, when man has forgotten that his only welfare lies in living after the likeness of God.

Not that I learnt the lesson then. When the first excitement of horror and wonder were past, what I had seen made me for years the veriest aristocrat, full of hatred and contempt of these dangerous classes, whose existence I had for the first time discovered. It required many years—years, too, of personal intercourse with the poor—to explain to me the true meaning of what I saw here in October twenty-seven years ago, and to learn a part of that lesson which God taught to others thereby. And one part at least of that lesson was this: That the social state of a city depends directly on its moral state, and—I fear dissenting voices, but I must say what I believe to be truth—that the moral state of a city depends—how far I know not, but frightfully, to an extent as yet uncalculated, and perhaps incalculable—on the physical state of that city; on the food, water, air, and lodging of its inhabitants.

But that lesson, and others connected with it, was learnt, and learnt well, by hundreds. From the sad catastrophe I date the rise of that interest in Social

Science; that desire for some nobler, more methodic, more permanent benevolence than that which stops at mere almsgiving and charity-schools. The dangerous classes began to be recognised as an awful fact which must be faced; and faced, not by repression, but by improvement. The "Perils of the Nation" began to occupy the attention not merely of politicians, but of philosophers, physicians, priests; and the admirable book which assumed that title did but re-echo the feeling of thousands of earnest hearts.

Ever since that time, scheme on scheme of improvement has been not only proposed but carried out. A general interest of the upper classes in the lower, a general desire to do good, and to learn how good can be done, has been awakened throughout England, such as, I boldly say, never before existed in any country upon earth; and England, her eyes opened to her neglect of these classes, without whose strong arms her wealth and genius would be useless, has put herself into a permanent state of confession of sin, repentance, and amendment, which I verily trust will be accepted by Almighty God; and will, in spite of our present shame and sorrow,[10] in spite of shame and sorrow which may be yet in store for us, save alive both the soul and the body of this ancient people.

Let us then, that we may learn how to bear our part in this great work of Social Reform, consider awhile great cities, their good and evil; and let us start from the facts about your own city of which I

---

10 This was spoken during the Indian Mutiny

have just put you in remembrance. The universal law will be best understood from the particular instance; and best of all, from the instance with which you are most intimately acquainted. And do not, I entreat you, fear that I shall be rude enough to say anything which may give pain to you, my generous hosts; or presumptuous enough to impute blame to anyone for events which happened long ago, and of the exciting causes of which I know little or nothing. Bristol was then merely in the same state in which other cities of England were, and in which every city on the Continent is now; and the local exciting causes of that outbreak, the personal conduct of A or B in it, is just what we ought most carefully to forget, if we wish to look at the real root of the matter. If consumption, latent in the constitution, have broken out in active mischief, the wise physician will trouble his head little with the particular accident which woke up the sleeping disease. The disease was there, and if one thing had not awakened it some other would. And so, if the population of a great city have got into a socially diseased state, it matters little what shock may have caused it to explode. Politics may in one case, fanaticism in another, national hatred in a third, hunger in a fourth—perhaps even, as in Byzantium of old, no more important matter than the jealousy between the blue and the green charioteers in the theatre, may inflame a whole population to madness and civil war. Our business is not with the nature of the igniting spark, but of the powder which is ignited.

I will not, then, to begin, go as far as some who say that "A great city is a great evil." We cannot say that Bristol was in 1830 or is now, a great evil. It represents so much realised wealth; and that, again, so much employment for thousands. It represents so much commerce; so much knowledge of foreign lands; so much distribution of their products; so much science, employed about that distribution.

And it is undeniable, that as yet we have had no means of rapid and cheap distribution of goods, whether imports or manufactures, save by this crowding of human beings into great cities, for the more easy despatch of business. Whether we shall devise other means hereafter is a question of which I shall speak presently. Meanwhile, no man is to be blamed for the existence, hardly even for the evils, of great cities. The process of their growth has been very simple. They have gathered themselves round abbeys and castles, for the sake of protection; round courts, for the sake of law; round ports, for the sake of commerce; round coal mines, for the sake of manufacture. Before the existence of railroads, penny-posts, electric telegraphs, men were compelled to be as close as possible to each other, in order to work together.

When the population was small, and commerce feeble, the cities grew to no very great size, and the bad effects of this crowding were not felt. The cities of England in the Middle Age were too small to keep their inhabitants week after week, month after month, in one deadly vapour-bath of foul gas; and though the mortality among infants was probably excessive, yet we should have seen among the adult survivors few or none of those stunted and etiolated figures so common now in England, as well as on the Continent. The green fields were close outside the walls, where lads and lasses went a-maying, and children gathered flowers, and sober burghers with their wives took the evening walk; there were the butts, too, close outside, where stalwart prentice-lads ran and wrestled, and pitched the bar, and played backsword, and practised with the long-bow; and sometimes, in stormy times, turned out for a few months as ready-trained soldiers, and, like Ulysses of old,

Drank delight of battle with their peers,

and then returned again to the workshop and the loom. The very mayor and alderman went forth, at five o'clock on the summer's morning, with hawk and leaping-pole, after a duck and heron; or hunted the hare in state, probably in the full glory of furred gown and gold chain; and then returned to breakfast, and doubtless transacted their day's business all the better for their morning's gallop on the breezy downs.

But there was another side to this genial and healthy picture. A hint that this was a state of society which had its conditions, its limit; and if those were infringed, woe alike to burgher and to prentice. Every now and then epidemic disease entered the jolly city—and then down went strong and weak, rich and poor, before the invisible and seemingly supernatural arrows of that angel of death whom they had been pampering unwittingly in every bedroom.

They fasted, they prayed; but in vain. They called the pestilence a judgment of God; and they called it by a true name. But they know not (and who are we to blame them for not knowing?) what it was that God was judging thereby—foul air, foul water, unclean backyards, stifling attics, houses hanging over the narrow street till light and air were alike shut out— that there lay the sin; and that to amend that was the repentance which God demanded.

Yet we cannot blame them. They showed that the crowded city life can bring out human nobleness as well as human baseness; that to be crushed into contact with their fellow-men, forced at least the loftier and tender souls to know their fellow-men, and therefore to care for them, to love them, to die for them. Yes— from one temptation the city life is free, to which the country life is sadly exposed—that isolation which, self-contented and self-helping, forgets in its surly independence that man is his brother's keeper. In cities, on the contrary, we find that the stories of these old pestilences, when the first panic terror has past, become, however tragical, still beautiful and heroic; and we read of noble-hearted men and women palliating ruin which they could not cure, braving dangers which seemed to them miraculous, from which they were utterly defenceless, spending money, time, and, after all, life itself upon sufferers from whom they might without shame have fled.

They are very cheering, the stories of the old city pestilences; and the nobleness which they brought out in the heart of many a townsman who had seemed absorbed in the lust of gain—who perhaps had been really absorbed in it—till that fearful hour awakened in him his better self, and taught him, not self-aggrandisement, but self-sacrifice; begetting in him, out of the very depth of darkness, new and divine light. That nobleness, doubt it not, exists as ever in the hearts of citizens. May God grant us to see the day when it shall awaken to exert itself, not for the palliation, not even for the cure, but for the prevention, yea, the utter extermination, of pestilence.

About the middle of the sixteenth century, as far as I can ascertain, another and even more painful phenomenon appears in our great cities—a dangerous class. How it arose is not yet clear. That the Reformation had something to do with the matter, we can hardly doubt. At the dissolution of the monasteries, the more idle, ignorant, and profligate members of the mendicant orders, unable to live any longer on the alms of the public, sunk, probably, into vicious penury. The frightful misgovernment of this country during the minority of Edward the Sixth, especially the conversion of tilled lands into pasture, had probably the effect of driving the surplus agricultural population into the great towns. But the social history of this whole period is as yet obscure, and I have no right to give an opinion on it. Another element, and a more potent one, is to be found in the discharged soldiers who came home from foreign war, and the sailors who returned from our voyages of discovery, and from our raids against the Spaniards, too often crippled by scurvy, or by Tropic fevers, with perhaps a little prize money, which was as hastily spent as it had been hastily gained. The later years of Elizabeth, and the whole of James the First's reign, disclose to us an ugly state of society in the low streets of all our seaport towns; and Bristol, as one of the great starting-points of West Indian adventure, was probably, during the seventeenth century, as bad as any city in England. According to Ben Jonson, and the playwriters of his time, the beggars become a regular fourth-estate, with their own laws, and even their own language— of which we may remark, that the thieves' Latin of those days is full of German words, indicating that its inventors had been employed in the Continental wars of the time. How that class sprung up, we may see, I suppose, pretty plainly, from Shakespeare's "Henry the Fifth." Whether Nym, Pistol, and Bardolph, Doll and Mrs. Quickly, existed in the reign of Henry the Fifth, they certainly existed in the reign of Elizabeth. They are probably sketches from life of people whom Shakespeare had seen in Alsatia and the Mint.

To these merely rascal elements, male and female, we must add, I fear, those whom mere penury, from sickness, failure, want of employment drove into dwellings of the lowest order. Such people, though not criminal themselves, are but too likely to become the parents of criminals. I am not blaming them, poor souls; God forbid! I am merely stating a fact. When we examine into the ultimate cause of a dangerous class; into the one property common to all its members, whether thieves, beggars, profligates, or the merely pauperised—we find it to be this loss of self-respect. As long as that remains, poor souls may struggle on heroically, pure amid penury, filth, degradation unspeakable. But when self-respect is lost, they are lost with it. And whatever may be the fate of virtuous parents, children brought up in dens of physical and moral filth cannot retrieve self-respect. They sink, they must sink, into a life on a level with the sights, sounds, aye, the very smells, which surround them. It is not merely that the child's mind is contaminated, by seeing and hearing, in overcrowded houses, what he should not hear and see: but the whole physical circumstances of his life are destructive of self-respect. He has no means for washing himself properly: but he has enough of the innate sense of beauty and fitness to feel that he ought not to be dirty; he thinks that others despise him for being dirty, and he half despises himself for being so. In all raged schools and reformatories, so they tell me, the first step toward restoring self-respect is to make the poor fellows clean. From that moment they begin to look on themselves as new men—with a new start, new hopes, new duties. For not without the deepest physical as well as moral meaning, was baptism chosen by the old Easterns, and adopted by our Lord Jesus Christ, as the sign of a new life; and outward purity made the token and symbol of that inward purity which is the parent of self-respect, and manliness, and a clear conscience; of the free forehead, and the eye which meets boldly and honestly the eye of its fellow-man.

But would that mere physical dirt were all that the lad has to contend with. There is the desire of enjoyment. Moral and intellectual enjoyment he has none, and can have none: but not to enjoy something is to be dead in life; and to the lowest physical pleasures he will betake himself, and all the more fiercely because his opportunities of enjoyment are so limited. It is a hideous subject; I will pass it by very shortly; only asking of you, as I have to ask daily of myself—this solemn question: We, who have so many comforts, so many pleasures of body, soul, and spirit, from the lowest appetite to the highest aspiration, that we can gratify each in turn with due and wholesome moderation, innocently and innocuously—who are we that we should judge the poor untaught and overtempted inhabitant of Temple Street and Lewin's Mead, if, having but one or two pleasures possible to him, he snatches greedily, even foully, at the little which he has?

And this brings me to another, and a most fearful evil of great cities, namely, drunkenness. I am one of those who cannot, on scientific grounds, consider drunkenness as a cause of evil, but as an effect. Of course it is a cause—a cause of endless crime and misery; but I am convinced that to cure, you must inquire, not what it causes, but what causes it? And for that we shall not have to seek far.

The main exciting cause of drunkenness is, I believe, firmly, bad air and bad lodging.

A man shall spend his days between a foul alley where he breathes sulphuretted hydrogen, a close workshop where he breathes carbonic acid, and a close and foul bedroom where he breathes both. In neither of the three places, meanwhile, has he his fair share of that mysterious chemical agent without which health is impossible, the want of which betrays itself at once in the dull eye, the sallow cheek—namely, light. Believe me, it is no mere poetic metaphor which connects in Scripture, Light with Life. It is the expression of a deep law, one which holds as true in the physical as in the spiritual world; a case in which (as perhaps in all cases) the laws of the visible world are the counterparts of those of the invisible world, and Earth is the symbol of Heaven.

Deprive, then, the man of his fair share of fresh air and pure light, and what follows? His blood is not properly oxygenated: his nervous energy is depressed, his digestion impaired, especially if his occupation be sedentary, or requires much stooping, and the cavity of the chest thereby becomes contracted; and for that miserable feeling of languor and craving he knows but one remedy—the passing stimulus of alcohol;— a passing stimulus; leaving fresh depression behind it, and requiring fresh doses of stimulant, till it becomes a habit, a slavery, a madness. Again, there is an intellectual side to the question. The depressed nervous energy, the impaired digestion, depress the spirits. The man feels low in mind as well as in body. Whence shall he seek exhilaration? Not in that stifling home which has caused the depression itself. He knows none other than the tavern, and the company which the tavern brings; God help him!

Yes, ladies and gentlemen, it is easy to say, God help him; but it is not difficult for man to help him also. Drunkenness is a very curable malady. The last fifty years has seen it all but die out among the upper classes of this country. And what has caused the improvement?

Certainly, in the first place, the spread of education. Every man has now a hundred means of rational occupation and amusement which were closed to his grandfather; and among the deadliest enemies of drunkenness, we may class the printing-press, the railroad, and the importation of foreign art and foreign science, which we owe to the late forty years' peace. We can find plenty of amusement now, beside the old one of sitting round the table and talking over wine. Why should not the poor man share in our gain? But over and above, there are causes simply physical. Our houses are better ventilated. The stifling old four-post bed has given place to the airy curtainless one; and what is more than all—we wash. That morning cold bath which foreigners consider as Young England's strangest superstition, has done as much, believe me, to abolish drunkenness, as any other cause whatsoever. With a clean skin in healthy action, and nerves and muscles braced by a sudden shock, men do not crave for artificial stimulants. I have found that, coeteris paribus, a man's sobriety is in direct proportion to his cleanliness. I believe it would be so in all classes had they the means.

And they ought to have the means. Whatever other rights a man has, or ought to have, this at least he has, if society demands of him that he should earn his own livelihood, and not be a torment and a burden to his neighbours. He has a right to water, to air, to light. In demanding that, he demands no more than nature has given to the wild beast of the forest. He is better than they. Treat him, then, as well as God has treated them. If we require of him to be a man, we must at least put him on a level with the brutes.

We have then, first of all, to face the existence of a dangerous class of this kind, into which the weaker as well as the worst members of society have a continual tendency to sink. A class which, not respecting itself, does not respect others; which has nothing to lose and all to gain by anarchy; in which the lowest passions, seldom gratified, are ready to burst out and avenge themselves by frightful methods.

For the reformation of that class, thousands of good men are now working; hundreds of benevolent plans are being set on foot. Honour to them all; whether they succeed or fail, each of them does some good; each of them rescues at least a few fellow-men, dear to God as you and I are, out of the nether pit. Honour to them all, I say; but I should not be honest with you this night, if I did not assert most solemnly my conviction, that reformatories, ragged schools, even hospitals and asylums, treat only the symptoms, not the actual causes, of the disease; and that the causes are only to be touched by improving the simple physical conditions of the class; by abolishing foul air, foul water, foul lodging, overcrowded dwellings, in which morality is difficult and common decency impossible. You may breed a pig in a sty, ladies and gentlemen, and make a learned pig of him after all; but you cannot breed a man in a sty, and make a learned man of him; or indeed, in the true sense of that great word, a man at all.

And remember, that these physical influences of great cities, physically depressing and morally degrading, influence, though to a less extent, the classes above the lowest stratum.

The honest and skilled workman feels their effects. Compelled too often to live where he can, in order to be near his work, he finds himself perpetually in contact with a class utterly inferior to himself, and his children exposed to contaminating influences from which he would gladly remove them; but how can he? Next door to him, even in the same house with him, may be enacted scenes of brutality or villainy which I will not speak of here. He may shut his own eyes and ears to them; but he cannot shut his children's. He may vex his righteous soul daily, like Lot of old, with the foul conversation of the wicked; but, like Lot of old, he cannot keep his children from mixing with the inhabitants of the wicked city, learning their works, and at last being involved in their doom. Oh, ladies and gentlemen, if there be one class for whom above all others I will plead, in season and out of season; if there be one social evil which I will din into the ears of my countrymen whenever God gives me a chance, it is this: The honest and the virtuous workman, and his unnatural contact with the dishonest and the foul. I know well the nobleness which exists in the average of that class, in men and in wives—their stern un-complaining, valorous self-denial; and nothing more stirs my pity than to see them struggling to bring up a family in a moral and physical atmosphere where right education is impossible. We lavish sympathy enough upon the criminal; for God's sake let us keep a little of it for the honest man. We spend thousands in car-rying out the separation of classes in prison; for God's sake let us try to separate them a little before they go to prison. We are afraid of the dangerous classes; for God's sake let us bestir ourselves to stop that reckless confusion and neglect which reign in the alleys and courts of our great towns, and which recruit those very dangerous classes from the class which ought to be, and is still, in spite of our folly, England's strength and England's glory. Let us no longer stand by idle, and see moral purity, in street after street, pent in the same noisome den with moral corruption, to be in-volved in one common doom, as the Latin tyrant of old used to bind together the dead corpse and the liv-ing victim. But let the man who would deserve well of his city, well of his country, set his heart and brain to the great purpose of giving the workmen dwellings fit for a virtuous and a civilised being, and like the priest of old, stand between the living and the dead, that the plague may be stayed.

Hardly less is the present physical state of our great cities felt by that numerous class which is, next to the employer, the most important in a city. I mean the shopmen, clerks, and all the men, principally young ones, who are employed exclusively in the work of distribution. I have a great respect, I may say affection, for this class. In Bristol I know nothing of them; save that, from what I hear, the clerks ought in general to have a better status here than in most cities. I am told that it is the practice here for merchants to take into their houses very young boys, and train them to their business; that this connection between employer and employed is hereditary, and that clerkships pass from father to son in the same family. I rejoice to hear it. It is pleasant to find anywhere a relic of the old patriarchal bond, the permanent nexus between master and man, which formed so important and so healthful an element of the ancient mercantile system. One would gladly overlook a little favouritism and nepotism, a little sticking square men into round holes, and of round men into square holes, for the sake of having a class of young clerks and employes who felt that their master's business was their business, his honour theirs, his prosperity theirs.

But over and above this, whenever I have come in contact with this clerk and shopman class, they have impressed me with considerable respect, not merely as to what they may be hereafter, but what they are now.

They are the class from which the ranks of our commercial men, our emigrants, are continually recruited; therefore their right education is a matter of national importance.

The lad who stands behind a Bristol counter may be, five-and-twenty years hence, a large employer—an owner of houses and land in far countries across the seas—a member of some colonial parliament—the founder of a wealthy family. How necessary for the honour of Britain, for the welfare of generations yet unborn, that that young man should have, in body, soul, and spirit, the loftiest, and yet the most practical of educations.

His education, too, such as it is, is one which makes me respect him as one of a class. Of course, he is sometimes one of those "gents" whom Punch so ruthlessly holds up to just ridicule. He is sometimes a vulgar fop, sometimes fond of low profligacy—of betting-houses and casinos. Well—I know no class in any age or country among which a fool may not be found here and there. But that the "gent" is the average type of this class, I should utterly deny from such experience as I have had. The peculiar note and mark of the average clerk and shopman, is, I think, in these days, intellectual activity, a keen desire for self-improvement and for independence, honourable, because self-acquired. But as he is distinctly a creature of the city; as all city influences bear at once on him more than on any other class, so we see in him, I think, more than in any class, the best and the worst effects of modern city life. The worst, of course, is low profligacy; but of that I do not speak here. I mean that in the same man the good and evil of a city life meet. And in this way.

In a countryman like me, coming up out of wild and silent moorlands into a great city, the first effect of the change is increased intellectual activity. The perpetual stream of human faces, the innumerable objects of interest in every shop-window, are enough to excite the mind to action, which is increased by the simple fact of speaking to fifty different human beings in the day instead of five. Now in the city-bred youth this excited state of mind is chronic, permanent. It is denoted plainly enough by the difference between the countryman's face and that of the townsman. The former in its best type (and it is often very noble) composed, silent, self-contained, often stately, often listless; the latter mobile, eager, observant, often brilliant, often self-conscious.

Now if you keep this rapid and tense mind in a powerful and healthy body, it would do right good work. Right good work it does, indeed, as it is; but still it might do better.

For what are the faults of this class? What do the obscurantists (now, thank God, fewer every day) allege as the objection to allowing young men to educate themselves out of working hours?

They become, it is said, discontented, conceited, dogmatical. They take up hasty notions, they condemn fiercely what they have no means of understanding;

they are too fond of fine words, of the excitement of spouting themselves, and hearing others spout.

Well. I suppose there must be a little truth in the accusation, or it would not have been invented. There is no smoke without fire; and these certainly are the faults of which the cleverest middle-class young men whom I know are most in danger.

But—one fair look at these men's faces ought to tell common sense that the cause is rather physical than moral. Confined to sedentary occupations, stooping over desks and counters in close rooms, unable to obtain that fair share of bodily exercise which nature demands, and in continual mental effort, their nerves and brain have been excited at the expense of their lungs, their digestion, and their whole nutritive system. Their complexions show a general ill-health. Their mouths, too often, hint at latent disease. What wonder if there be an irritability of brain and nerve? I blame them no more for it than I blame a man for being somewhat touchy while he is writhing in the gout. Indeed less; for gout is very often a man's own fault; but these men's ill-health is not. And, therefore, everything which can restore to them health of body, will preserve in them health of mind. Everything which ministers to the *corpus sanum,* will minister also to the *mentem sanam;* and a walk on Durham Downs, a game of cricket, a steamer excursion to Chepstow, shall send them home again happier and wiser men than poring over many wise volumes or hearing many wise lectures. How often is a worthy fellow spending his leisure honourably in hard reading, when he had much better have been scrambling over hedge and ditch, without a thought in his head save what was put there by the grass and the butterflies, and the green trees and the blue sky? And therefore I do press earnestly, both on employers and employed, the incalculable value of athletic sports and country walks for those whose business compels them to pass the day in the heart of the city; I press on you, with my whole soul, the excellency of the early-closing movement; not so much because it enables young men to attend mechanics' institutes, as because it enables them, if they choose, to get a good game of leap-frog. You may smile; but try the experiment, and see how, as the chest expands, the muscles harden, and the cheek grows ruddy and the lips firm, and sound sleep refreshes the lad for his next day's work, the temper will become more patient, the spirits more genial; there will be less tendency to brood angrily over the inequalities of fortune, and to accuse society for evils which as yet she knows not how to cure.

There is a class, again, above all these, which is doubtless the most important of all; and yet of which I can say little here—the capitalist, small and great, from the shopkeeper to the merchant prince.

Heaven forbid that I should speak of them with aught but respect. There are few figures, indeed, in the world on which I look with higher satisfaction than on the British merchant; the man whose ships are on a hundred seas; who sends comfort and

prosperity to tribes whom he never saw, and honourably enriches himself by enriching others. There is
something to me chivalrous, even kingly, in the merchant life; and there were men in Bristol of old—as
I doubt not there are now—who nobly fulfilled that
ideal. I cannot forget that Bristol was the nurse of
America; that more than two hundred years ago, the
daring and genius of Bristol converted yonder narrow stream into a mighty artery, down which flowed
the young life-blood of that great Transatlantic nation
destined to be hereafter, I believe, the greatest which
the world ever saw. Yes—were I asked to sum up in
one sentence the good of great cities, I would point
first to Bristol, and then to the United States, and say,
That is what great cities can do. By concentrating in
one place, and upon one object, men, genius, information, and wealth, they can conquer new-found lands
by arts instead of arms; they can beget new nations;
and replenish and subdue the earth from pole to pole.

Meanwhile, there is one fact about employers, in
all cities which I know, which may seem commonplace to you, but which to me is very significant.
Whatsoever business they may do in the city, they
take good care, if possible, not to live in it. As soon
as a man gets wealthy nowadays, his first act is to
take to himself a villa in the country. Do I blame
him? Certainly not. It is an act of common sense. He
finds that the harder he works, the more he needs of
fresh air, free country life, innocent recreation; and
he takes it, and does his city business all the better for

it, lives all the longer for it, is the cheerfuller, more genial man for it. One great social blessing, I think, which railroads have brought, is the throwing open country life to men of business. I say blessing; both to the men themselves and to the country where they settle. The citizen takes an honest pride in rivalling the old country gentleman, in beating him in his own sphere, as gardener, agriculturist, sportsman, head of the village; and by his superior business habits and his command of ready money, he very often does so. For fifty miles round London, wherever I see progress— improved farms, model cottages, new churches, new schools—I find, in three cases out of four, that the author is some citizen who fifty years ago would have known nothing but the narrow city life, and have had probably no higher pleasures than those of the table; whose dreams would have been, not as now, of model farms and schools, but of turtle and port-wine.

My only regret when I see so pleasant a sight is: Oh that the good man could have taken his workmen with him!

Taken his workmen with him?

I assure you that, after years of thought, I see no other remedy for the worst evils of city life. "If," says the old proverb, "the mountain will not come to Muhammed, then Muhammed must go to the mountain." And if you cannot bring the country into the city, the city must go into the country.

Do not fancy me a dreamer dealing with impossible ideals. I know well what cannot be done; fair and grand as it would be, if it were done, a model city is impossible in England. We have here no Eastern despotism (and it is well we have not) to destroy an old Babylon, as that mighty genius Nabuchonosor did, and build a few miles off a new Babylon, one-half the area of which was park and garden, fountain and water-course—a diviner work of art, to my mind, than the finest picture or statue which the world ever saw. We have not either (and it is well for us that we have not) a model republic occupying a new uncleared land. We cannot, as they do in America, plan out a vast city on some delicious and healthy site amid the virgin forest, with streets one hundred feet in breadth, squares and boulevards already planted by God's hand with majestic trees; and then leave the great design to be hewn out of the wilderness, street after street, square after square, by generations yet unborn. That too is a magnificent ideal; but it cannot be ours. And it is well for us, I believe, that it cannot. The great value of land, the enormous amount of vested interests, the necessity of keeping to ancient sites around which labour, as in Manchester, or commerce, as in Bristol, has clustered itself on account of natural advantages, all these things make any attempts to rebuild in cities impossible. But they will cause us at last, I believe, to build better things than cities. They will issue in a complete interpenetration of city and of country, a complete fusion of their different modes of life, and a combination of the advantages of both, such as no country in the world has ever seen. We shall have, I believe and trust, ere another generation has past, model lodging-houses springing up, not in the heart of the town, but on the hills around it; and those will be—economy, as well as science and good government, will compel them to be—not ill-built rows of undrained cottages, each rented for awhile, and then left to run into squalidity and disrepair, but huge blocks of building, each with its common eating-house, bar, baths, washhouses, reading-room, common conveniences of every kind, where, in free and pure country air, the workman will enjoy comforts which our own grandfathers could not command, and at a lower price than that which he now pays for such accommodation as I should be ashamed to give to my own horses; while from these great blocks of building, branch lines will convey the men to or from their work by railroad, without loss of time, labour, or health.

Then the city will become what it ought to be; the workshop, and not the dwelling-house, of a mighty and healthy people. The old foul alleys, as they become gradually depopulated, will be replaced by fresh warehouses, fresh public buildings; and the city, in spite of all its smoke and dirt, will become a place on which the workman will look down with pride and joy, because it will be to him no longer a prison and a poison-trap, but merely a place for honest labour.

This, gentlemen and ladies, is my ideal; and I cannot but hope and believe that I shall live to see it realised here and there, gradually and cautiously (as is our good and safe English habit), but still earnestly and well. Did I see but the movement commenced in earnest, I should be inclined to cry a "Nunc Domine dimittis"—I have lived long enough to see a noble work begun, which cannot but go on and prosper, so beneficial would it be found. I tell you, that but this afternoon, as the Bath train dashed through the last cutting, and your noble vale and noble city opened before me, I looked round upon the overhanging crags, the wooded glens, and said to myself: There, upon the rock in the free air and sunlight, and not here, beneath yon pall of smoke by the lazy pools and festering tidal muds, ought the Bristol workman to live. Oh that I may see the time when on the blessed Sabbath eve these hills shall swarm as thick with living men as bean-fields with the summer bees; when the glens shall ring with the laughter of ten thousand children, with limbs as steady, and cheeks as ruddy, as those of my own lads and lasses at home; and the artisan shall find his Sabbath a day of rest indeed, in which not only soul but body may gather health and nerve for the week's work, under the soothing and purifying influences of those common natural sights and sounds which God has given as a heritage even to the gipsy on the moor; and of which no man can be deprived without making his life a burden to himself, perhaps a burden to those around him.

But it will be asked: Will such improvements pay? I respect that question. I do not sneer at it, and regard it, as some are too apt to do, as a sign of the mercenary and money-loving spirit of the present age. I look on it as a healthy sign of the English mind; a sign that we believe, as the old Jews did, that political and social righteousness is inseparably connected with wealth and prosperity. The old Psalms and prophets have taught us that lesson; and God forbid that we should forget it. The world is right well made; and the laws of trade and of social economy, just as much as the laws of nature, are divine facts, and only by obeying them can we thrive. And I had far sooner hear a people asking of every scheme of good, Will it pay? than throwing themselves headlong into that merely sentimental charity to which superstitious nations have always been prone—charity which effects no permanent good, which, whether in Hindostan or in Italy, debases, instead of raising, the suffering classes, because it breaks the laws of social economy.

No, let us still believe that if a thing is right, it will sooner or later pay; and in social questions, make the profitableness of any scheme a test of its rightness. It is a rough test; not an infallible one at all, but it is a fair one enough to work by.

And as for the improvements at which I have hinted, I will boldly answer that they will pay.

They will pay directly and at once, in the saving of poor-rates. They will pay by exterminating epidemics, and numberless chronic forms of disease which now render thousands burdens on the public purse; consumers, instead of producers of wealth. They will pay by gradually absorbing the dangerous classes; and removing from temptation and degradation a generation yet unborn. They will pay in the increased content, cheerfulness, which comes with health in increased goodwill of employed towards employers. They will pay by putting the masses into a state fit for education. They will pay, too, in such fearful times as these, by the increased physical strength and hardihood of the town populations. For it is from the city, rather than from the country, that our armies must mainly be recruited. Not only is the townsman more ready to enlist than the countryman, because in the town the labour market is most likely to be overstocked; but the townsman actually makes a better soldier than the countryman. He is a shrewder, more active, more self-helping man; give him but the chances of maintaining the same physical strength and health as the countryman, and he will support the honour of the British arms as gallantly as the Highlander or the Connaughtman, and restore the days when the invincible prentice-boys of London carried terror into the heart of foreign lands. In all ages, in all times, whether for war or for peace, it will pay. The true wealth of a nation is the health of her masses.

It may seem to some here that I have dealt too much throughout this lecture with merely material questions; that I ought to have spoken more of intellectual progress; perhaps, as a clergyman, more also of spiritual and moral regeneration.

I can only answer, that if this be a fault on my part, it is a deliberate one. I have spoken, whether rightly or wrongly, concerning what I know—concerning matters which are to me articles of faith altogether indubitable, irreversible, Divine.

Be it that these are merely questions of physical improvement. I see no reason in that why they should be left to laymen, or urged only on worldly grounds and self-interest. I do not find that when urged on those grounds, the advice is listened to. I believe that it will not be listened to until the consciences of men, as well as their brains, are engaged in these questions; until they are put on moral grounds, shown to have connection with moral laws; and so made questions not merely of interest, but of duty, honour, chivalry.

I cannot but see, moreover, how many phenomena, which are supposed to be spiritual, are simply physical; how many cases which are referred to my profession, are properly the object of the medical man. I cannot but see, that unless there be healthy bodies, it is impossible in the long run to have a generation of healthy souls; I cannot but see that mankind are as prone now as ever to deny the sacredness and perfection of God's physical universe, as an excuse for their own ignorance and neglect thereof; to search the highest heaven for causes which lie patent at their feet, and like the heathen of old time, to impute to some capricious anger of the gods calamities which spring from their own greed, haste, and ignorance.

And, therefore, because I am a priest, and glory in the name of a priest, I have tried to fulfil somewhat of that which seems to me the true office of a priest—namely, to proclaim to man the Divine element which exists in all, even the smallest thing, because each thing is a thought of God himself; to make men understand that God is indeed about their path and about their bed, spying out all their ways; that they are indeed fearfully and wonderfully made, and that God's hand lies for ever on them, in the form of physical laws, sacred, irreversible, universal, reaching from one end of the universe to the other; that whosoever persists in breaking those laws, reaps his sure punishment of weakness and sickness, sadness and self-reproach; that whosoever causes them to be broken by others, reaps his sure punishment in finding that he has transformed his fellow-men into burdens and curses, instead of helpmates and blessings. To say this, is a priest's duty; and then to preach the good news that the remedy is patent, easy, close at hand; that many of the worst evils which afflict humanity may be exterminated by simple common sense, and the justice and mercy which does to others as it would be done by; to awaken men to the importance of the visible world, that they may judge from thence the higher importance of that invisible world whereof this is but the garment and the type; and in all times and places, instead of keeping the key of knowledge to pamper one's own power or pride, to lay that key frankly and trustfully in the hand of every human being who hungers after truth, and to say: Child of God, this key is thine as well as mine. Enter boldly into thy Father's house, and behold the wonder, the wisdom, the beauty of its laws and its organisms, from the mightiest planet over thy head, to the tiniest insect beneath thy feet. Look at it, trustfully, joyfully, earnestly; for it is thy heritage. Behold its perfect fitness for thy life here; and judge from thence its fitness for thy nobler life hereafter.

HEROISM

It is an open question whether the policeman is not demoralising us; and that in proportion as he does his duty well; whether the perfection of justice and safety, the complete "preservation of body and goods," may not reduce the educated and comfortable classes into that lap-dog condition in which not conscience, but comfort, doth make cowards of us all. Our forefathers had, on the whole, to take care of themselves; we find it more convenient to hire people to take care of us. So much the better for us, in some respects; but, it may be, so much the worse in others. So much the better; because, as usually results from the division of labour, these people, having little or nothing to do save to take care of us, do so far better than we could; and so prevent a vast amount of violence and wrong, and therefore of misery, especially to the weak; for which last reason we will acquiesce in the existence of policemen and lawyers, as we do in the results of arbitration, as the lesser of two evils. The odds in war are in favour of the bigger bully, in arbitration in favour of the bigger rogue; and it is a question whether the lion or the fox be the safer guardian of human interests. But arbitration prevents war; and that, in three cases out of four, is full reason for employing it.

On the other hand, the lap-dog condition, whether in dogs or in men, is certainly unfavourable to the growth of the higher virtues. Safety and comfort are good, indeed, for the good; for the brave, the self-originating, the earnest. They give to such a clear stage and no favour, wherein to work unhindered for their fellow-men. But for the majority, who are neither brave, self-originating, nor earnest, but the mere puppets of circumstance, safety and comfort may, and actually do, merely make their lives mean and petty, effeminate and dull. Therefore their hearts must be awakened, as often as possible, to take exercise enough for health; and they must be reminded, perpetually and importunately, of what a certain great philosopher called, "whatsoever things are true, honourable, just, pure, lovely, and of good report;" "if there be any manhood, and any just praise, to think of such things."

This pettiness and dulness of our modern life is just what keeps alive our stage, to which people go to see something a little less petty, a little less dull, than what they see at home. It is, too, the cause of—I had almost said the excuse for—the modern rage for sensational novels. Those who read them so greedily are conscious, poor souls, of capacities in themselves of passion and action for good and evil, for which their frivolous humdrum daily life gives no room, no vent.

They know too well that human nature can be more fertile, whether in weeds and poisons, or in flowers and fruits, than it is usually in the streets and houses of a well-ordered and tolerably sober city. And because the study of human nature is, after all, that which is nearest to everyone and most interesting to everyone, therefore they go to fiction, since they cannot go to fact, to see what they themselves might be had they the chance; to see what fantastic tricks before high heaven men and women like themselves can play, and how they play them.

Well, it is not for me to judge, for me to blame. I will only say that there are those who cannot read sensational novels, or, indeed, any novels at all, just because they see so many sensational novels being enacted round them in painful facts of sinful flesh and blood. There are those, too, who have looked in the mirror too often to wish to see their own disfigured visage in it any more; who are too tired of themselves and ashamed of themselves to want to hear of people like themselves; who want to hear of people utterly unlike themselves, more noble, and able, and just, and sweet, and pure; who long to hear of heroism and to converse with heroes; and who, if by chance they meet with an heroic act, bathe their spirits in that, as in May-dew, and feel themselves thereby, if but for an hour, more fair.

If any such shall chance to see these words, let me ask them to consider with me that one word Hero, and what it means.

Hero; Heroic; Heroism. These words point to a phase of human nature, the capacity for which we all have in ourselves, which is as startling and as interesting in its manifestations as any, and which is always beautiful, always ennobling, and therefore always attractive to those whose hearts are not yet seared by the world or brutalised by self-indulgence.

But let us first be sure what the words mean. There is no use talking about a word till we have got at its meaning. We may use it as a cant phrase, as a party cry on platforms; we may even hate and persecute our fellow-men for the sake of it: but till we have clearly settled in our own minds what a word means, it will do for fighting with, but not for working with. Socrates of old used to tell the young Athenians that the ground of all sound knowledge was—to understand the true meaning of the words which were in their mouths all day long; and Socrates was a wiser man than we shall ever see. So, instead of beginning an oration in praise of heroism, I shall ask my readers to think with me what heroism is.

Now, we shall always get most surely at the meaning of a word by getting at its etymology—that is, at what it meant at first. And if heroism means behaving like a hero, we must find out, it seems to me, not merely what a hero may happen to mean just now, but what it meant in the earliest human speech in which we find it.

A hero or a heroine, then, among the old Homeric Greeks, meant a man or woman who was like the gods; and who, from that likeness, stood superior to his or her fellow-creatures. Gods, heroes, and men, is a threefold division of rational beings, with which we meet more than once or twice. Those grand old Greeks felt deeply the truth of the poet's saying—

Unless above himself he can
Exalt himself, how poor a thing is man.

But more: the Greeks supposed these heroes to be, in some way or other, partakers of a divine nature; akin to the gods; usually, either they, or some ancestor of theirs, descended from a god or goddess. Those who have read Mr. Gladstone's "Juventus Mundi" will remember the section (cap. ix. 6) on the modes of the approximation between the divine and the human natures; and whether or not they agree with the author altogether, all will agree, I think, that the first idea of a hero or a heroine was a godlike man or godlike woman.

A godlike man. What varied, what infinite forms of nobleness that word might include, ever increasing, as men's notions of the gods became purer and loftier, or, alas! decreasing, as their notions became degraded. The old Greeks, with that intense admiration of beauty which made them, in after ages, the master-sculptors and draughtsmen of their own, and, indeed, of any age, would, of course, require in their hero, their god-like man, beauty and strength, manners too, and eloquence, and all outward perfections of humanity, and neglect his moral qualities. Neglect, I say, but not ignore. The hero, by virtue of his kindred with the gods, was always expected to be a better man than common men, as virtue was then understood. And how better? Let us see.

The hero was at least expected to be more reverent than other men to those divine beings of whose nature he partook, whose society he might enjoy even here on earth. He might be unfaithful to his own high lineage; he might misuse his gifts by selfishness and self-will; he might, like Ajax, rage with mere jealousy and wounded pride till his rage ended in shameful madness and suicide. He might rebel against the very gods, and all laws of right and wrong, till he perished his ἀυασθαλίη—

Smitten down, blind in his pride, for a sign and
a terror to mortals.

But he ought to have, he must have, to be true to his name of Hero, justice, self-restraint, and αἰδὼς— that highest form of modesty, for which we have, alas! no name in the English tongue; that perfect respect for the feelings of others which springs out of perfect self-respect. And he must have too—if he were to be a hero of the highest type—the instinct of helpfulness; the instinct that, if he were a kinsman of the gods, he must fight on their side, through toil and danger, against all that was unlike them, and therefore hateful to them. Who loves not the old legends, unsurpassed for beauty in the literature of any race, in which the hero stands out as the deliverer, the destroyer of evil? Theseus ridding the land of robbers, and delivering it

from the yearly tribute of boys and maidens to be de-
voured by the Minotaur; Perseus slaying the Gorgon,
and rescuing Andromeda from the sea-beast; Hera-
cles with his twelve famous labours against giants and
monsters; and all the rest—

> *Who dared, in the god-given might of their manhood,*
> *Greatly to do and to suffer, and far in the fens and*
> *the forests*
> *Smite the devourers of men, heaven-hated brood of*
> *the giants;*
> *Transformed, strange, without like, who obey not the*
> *golden-haired rulers.*

These are figures whose divine moral beauty has
sunk into the hearts, not merely of poets or of artists,
but of men and women who suffered and who feared;
the memory of them, fables though they may have
been, ennobled the old Greek heart; they ennobled
the heart of Europe in the fifteenth century, at the
re-discovery of Greek literature. So far from contra-
dicting the Christian ideal, they harmonised with—I
had almost said they supplemented—that more tender and saintly ideal of heroism which had sprung
up during the earlier Middle Ages. They justified,
and actually gave a new life to, the old noblenesses
of chivalry, which had grown up in the later Middle
Ages as a necessary supplement of active and manly
virtue to the passive and feminine virtue of the clois-
ter. They inspired, mingling with these two other elements, a literature both in England, France, and Italy,

in which the three elements, the saintly, the chivalrous, and the Greek heroic, have become one and undistinguishable, because all three are human, and all three divine; a literature which developed itself in Ariosto, in Tasso, in the Hypnerotomachia, the Arcadia, the Euphues, and other forms, sometimes fantastic, sometimes questionable, but which reached its perfection in our own Spenser's "Fairy Queen"—perhaps the most admirable poem which has ever been penned by mortal man.

And why? What has made these old Greek myths live, myths though they be, and fables, and fair dreams? What—though they have no body, and, perhaps, never had—has given them an immortal soul, which can speak to the immortal souls of all generations to come?

What but this, that in them—dim it may be and undeveloped, but still there—lies the divine idea of self-sacrifice as the perfection of heroism, of self-sacrifice, as the highest duty and the highest joy of him who claims a kindred with the gods?

Let us say, then, that true heroism must involve self-sacrifice. Those stories certainly involve it, whether ancient or modern, which the hearts, not of philosophers merely, or poets, but of the poorest and the most ignorant, have accepted instinctively as the highest form of moral beauty—the highest form, and yet one possible to all.

Grace Darling rowing out into the storm towards the wreck. The "drunken private of the Buffs," who, prisoner among the Chinese, and commanded to prostrate himself and kotoo, refused in the name of his country's honour: "He would not bow to any Chinaman on earth:" and so was knocked on the head, and died surely a hero's death. Those soldiers of the Birkenhead, keeping their ranks to let the women and children escape, while they watched the sharks who in a few minutes would be tearing them limb from limb. Or, to go across the Atlantic—for there are heroes in the Far West—Mr. Bret Harte's "Flynn of Virginia," on the Central Pacific Railway—the place is shown to travellers—who sacrificed his life for his married comrade:

There, in the drift,
Back to the wall,
He held the timbers
Ready to fall.
Then in the darkness
I heard him call:
"Run for your life, Jake!
Run for your wife's sake!
Don't wait for me."

And that was all
Heard in the din—
Heard of Tom Flynn—
Flynn of Virginia.

Or the engineer, again, on the Mississippi, who, when the steamer caught fire, held, as he had sworn he would, her bow against the bank, till every soul save he got safe on shore:

Through the hot black breath of the burning boat
Jim Bludso's voice was heard;
And they all had trust in his cussedness,
And knew he would keep his word.
And sure's you're born, they all got off
Afore the smokestacks fell;
And Bludso's ghost went up alone
In the smoke of the Prairie Belle.

He weren't no saint—but at the judgment
I'd run my chance with Jim
Longside of some pious gentlemen
That wouldn't shake hands with him.
He'd seen his duty—a dead sure thing—
And went for it there and then;
And Christ is not going to be too hard
On a man that died for men'.

To which gallant poem of Colonel John Hay's—and he has written many gallant and beautiful poems—I have but one demurrer: Jim Bludso did not merely do his duty but more than his duty. He did a voluntary deed, to which he was bound by no code or contract, civil or moral; just as he who introduced me to that poem won his Victoria Cross—as many a cross, Victoria and other, has been won—by volunteering for a deed to which he, too, was bound by no code or contract, military or moral. And it is of the essence of self-sacrifice, and therefore of heroism, that it should be voluntary; a work of supererogation, at least towards society and man; an act to which the hero or heroine is not bound by duty, but which is above though not against duty.

Nay, on the strength of that same element of self-sacrifice, I will not grudge the epithet "heroic," which my revered friend Mr. Darwin justly applies to the poor little monkey, who once in his life did that which was above his duty; who lived in continual terror of the great baboon, and yet, when the brute had sprung upon his friend the keeper, and was tearing out his throat, conquered his fear by love, and, at the risk of instant death, sprang in turn upon his dreaded enemy, and bit and shrieked till help arrived.

Some would nowadays use that story merely to prove that the monkey's nature and the man's nature are, after all, one and the same. Well: I, at least, have never denied that there is a monkey-nature in man, as there is a peacock-nature, and a swine-nature, and a wolf-nature—of all which four I see every day too much. The sharp and stern distinction between men and animals, as far as their natures are concerned, is of a more modern origin than people fancy. Of old the Assyrian took the eagle, the ox, and the lion—and not unwisely—as the three highest types of human capacity. The horses of Homer might be immortal, and weep for their master's death. The animals and monsters of Greek myth—like the Ananzi spider of Negro fable—glide insensibly into speech and reason. Birds—the most wonderful of all animals in the eyes of a man of science or a poet—are sometimes looked on as wiser, and nearer to the gods, than man.

The Norseman—the noblest and ablest human being, save the Greek, of whom history can tell us—was not ashamed to say of the bear of his native forests that he had "ten men's strength and eleven men's wisdom." How could Reinecke Fuchs have gained immortality, in the Middle Ages and since, save by the truth of its too solid and humiliating theorem—that the actions of the world of men were, on the whole, guided by passions but too exactly like those of the lower animals? I have said, and say again, with good old Vaughan:

Unless above himself he can
Exalt himself, how mean a thing is man.

But I cannot forget that many an old Greek poet or sage, and many a sixteenth and seventeenth century one, would have interpreted the monkey's heroism from quite a different point of view; and would have said that the poor little creature had been visited suddenly by some "divine afflatus"—an expression quite as philosophical and quite as intelligible as most philosophic formulas which I read nowadays—and had been thus raised for the moment above his abject selfish monkey-nature, just as man requires to be raised above his. But that theory belongs to a philosophy which is out of date and out of fashion, and which will have to wait a century or two before it comes into fashion again.

And now, if self-sacrifice and heroism be, as I believe, identical, I must protest against the use of the word "sacrifice" which is growing too common in newspaper-columns, in which we are told of an "enormous sacrifice of life;" an expression which means merely that a great many poor wretches have been killed, quite against their own will, and for no purpose whatsoever; no sacrifice at all, unless it be one to the demons of ignorance, cupidity, or mismanagement.

The stout Whig undergraduate understood better the meaning of such words, who, when asked, "In what sense might Charles the First be said to be a martyr?" answered, "In the same sense that a man might be said to be a martyr to the gout."

And I must protest, in like wise, against a misuse of the words "hero." "heroism," "heroic," which is becoming too common, namely, applying them to mere courage. We have borrowed the misuse, I believe, as we have more than one beside, from the French press. I trust that we shall neither accept it, nor the temper which inspires it. It may be convenient for those who flatter their nation, and especially the military part of it, into a ruinous self-conceit, to frame some such syllogism as this: "Courage is heroism: every Frenchman is naturally courageous: therefore every Frenchman is a hero." But we, who have been trained at once in a sounder school of morals, and in a greater respect for facts, and for language as the expression of facts, shall be careful, I hope, not to trifle thus with that potent and awful engine—human speech. We shall eschew likewise, I hope, a like abuse of the word "moral," which has crept from the French press now and then, not only into our own press, but into the writings of some of our military men, who, as Englishmen, should have known better. We were told again and again, during the late war, that the moral effect of such a success had been great; that the *morale* of the troops was excellent; or again, that the *morale* of the troops had suffered, or even that they were somewhat demoralised. But when one came to test what was really meant by these fine words, one discovered that morals had nothing to do with the facts which they expressed; that the troops were in the one case actuated simply by the animal passion of hope, in the other simply by the animal passion of fear. This abuse of the word "moral" has crossed, I am sorry to say, the Atlantic; and a witty American, whom we must excuse, though we must not imitate, when some one had been blazing away at him with a revolver, he being unarmed, is said to have described his very natural emotions on the occasion, by saying that he felt dreadfully demoralised. We, I hope, shall confine the word "demoralisation," as our generals of the last century would have done, when applied to soldiers, to crime, including, of course, the neglect of duty or of discipline; and we shall mean by the word "heroism," in like manner, whether applied to a soldier or to any human being, not mere courage, not the mere doing of duty, but the doing of something beyond duty; something which is not in the bond; some spontaneous and unexpected act of self-devotion.

I am glad, but not surprised, to see that Miss Yonge has held to this sound distinction in her golden little book of "Golden Deeds," and said, "Obedience, at all costs and risks, is the very essence of a soldier's life. It has the solid material, but it has hardly the exceptional brightness, of a golden deed."

I know that it is very difficult to draw the line between mere obedience to duty and express heroism. I know also that it would be both invidious and impertinent in an utterly unheroic personage like me, to try to draw that line; and to sit at home at ease, analysing and criticising deeds which I could not do myself; but—to give an instance or two of what I mean:

To defend a post as long as it is tenable is not heroic. It is simple duty. To defend it after it has become untenable, and even to die in so doing, is not heroic, but a noble madness, unless an advantage is to be gained thereby for one's own side. Then, indeed, it rises towards, if not into, the heroism of self-sacrifice.

Who, for example, will not endorse the verdict of all ages on the conduct of those Spartans at Thermopylae, when they sat "combing their yellow hair for death" on the sea-shore? They devoted themselves to hopeless destruction; but why? They felt—I must believe that, for they behaved as if they felt—that on them the destinies of the Western World might hang; that they were in the forefront of the battle between civilisation and barbarism, between freedom and despotism; and that they must teach that vast mob of Persian slaves, whom the officers of the Great King were driving with whips up to their lance-points, that the spirit of the old heroes was not dead; and that the Greek, even in defeat and death, was a mightier and a nobler man than they. And they did their work. They produced, if you will, a "moral" effect, which has lasted even to this very day. They struck terror into the heart, not only of the Persian host, but of the whole Persian empire. They made the event of that war certain, and the victories of Salamis and Platæa comparatively easy. They made Alexander's conquest of the East, one hundred and fifty years afterwards, not only possible at all, but permanent when it came; and thus helped to determine the future civilisation of the whole world.

They did not, of course, foresee all this. No great or inspired man can foresee all the consequences of his deeds; but these men were, as I hold inspired to see somewhat at least of the mighty stake for which they played; and to count their lives worthless, if Sparta had sent them thither to help in that great game.

Or shall we refuse the name of heroic to those three German cavalry regiments who, in the battle of Mars-la-Tour, were bidden to hurl themselves upon the chassepots and mitrailleuses of the unbroken French infantry, and went to almost certain death, over the corpses of their comrades, on and in and through, reeling man over horse, horse over man, and clung like bull-dogs to their work, and would hardly leave, even at the bugle-call, till in one regiment thirteen officers out of nineteen were killed or wounded? And why?

Because the French army must be stopped, if it were but for a quarter of an hour. A respite must be gained for the exhausted Third Corps. And how much might be done, even in a quarter of an hour, by men who knew when, and where, and why to die! Who will refuse the name of heroes to these men? And yet they, probably, would have utterly declined the honour. They had but done that which was in the bond. They were but obeying orders after all. As Miss Yonge well says of all heroic persons: "'I have but done that which it was my duty to do,' is the natural answer of those capable of such actions. They have been constrained to them by duty or pity; have never deemed it possible to act otherwise; and did not once think of themselves in the matter at all."

These last true words bring us to another element in heroism: its simplicity. Whatsoever is not simple; whatsoever is affected, boastful, wilful, covetous, tarnishes, even destroys, the heroic character of a deed; because all these faults spring out of self. On the other hand, wherever you find a perfectly simple, frank, unconscious character, there you have the possibility, at least, of heroic action. For it is nobler far to do the most commonplace duty in the household, or behind the counter, with a single eye to duty, simply because it must be done—nobler far, I say, than to go out of your way to attempt a brilliant deed, with a double mind, and saying to yourself not only—"This will be a brilliant deed," but also—"and it will pay me, or raise me, or set me off, into the bargain." Heroism knows no "into the bargain." And therefore, again, I must protest against applying the word "heroic" to any deeds, however charitable, however toilsome, however dangerous, performed for the sake of what certain French ladies, I am told, call "faire son salut"—saving one's soul in the world to come. I do not mean to judge. Other and quite unselfish motives may be, and doubtless often are, mixed up with that selfish one: womanly pity and tenderness; love for, and desire to imitate, a certain Incarnate ideal of self-sacrifice, who is at once human and divine. But that motive of saving the soul, which is too often openly proposed and proffered, is utterly unheroic. The desire to escape pains and penalties hereafter by pains and penalties here; the balance of present loss against future gain—what is this but selfishness extended out of this world into eternity? "Not worldliness," indeed, as a satirist once said with bitter truth, "but other-worldliness."

Moreover—and the young and the enthusiastic should also bear this in mind—though heroism means the going beyond the limits of strict duty, it never means the going out of the path of strict duty. If it is your duty to go to London, go thither: you may go as much farther as you choose after that. But you must go to London first. Do your duty first; it will be time after that to talk of being heroic.

And therefore one must seriously warn the young, lest they mistake for heroism and self-sacrifice what is merely pride and self-will, discontent with the relations by which God has bound them, and the circumstances which God has appointed for them. I have known girls think they were doing a fine thing by leaving uncongenial parents or disagreeable sisters, and cutting out for themselves, as they fancied, a more useful and elevated line of life than that of mere home duties; while, after all, poor things, they were only saying, with the Pharisees of old, "Corban, it is a gift, by whatsoever thou mightest be profited by me;" and in the name of God, neglecting the command of God to honour their father and mother.

There are men, too, who will neglect their households and leave their children unprovided for, and even uneducated, while they are spending their money on philanthropic or religious hobbies of their own. It is ill to take the children's bread and cast it to the dogs; or even to the angels. It is ill, I say, trying to make presents to God, before we have tried to pay our debts to God. The first duty of every man is to the wife whom he has married, and to the children whom she has brought into the world; and to neglect them is not heroism, but self-conceit; the conceit that a man is so necessary to Almighty God, that God will actually allow him to do wrong, if He can only thereby secure the man's invaluable services. Be sure that every motive which comes not from the single eye, every motive which springs from self, is by its very essence unheroic, let it look as gaudy or as beneficent as it may.

But I cannot go so far as to say the same of the love of approbation—the desire for the love and respect of our fellow-men. That must not be excluded from the list of heroic motives. I know that it is, or may be proved to be, by victorious analysis, an emotion common to us and the lower animals. And yet no man excludes it less than that true hero, St. Paul.

If those brave Spartans, if those brave Germans, of whom I spoke just now, knew that their memories would be wept over and worshipped by brave men and fair women, and that their names would become watchwords to children in their fatherland, what is that to us, save that it should make us rejoice, if we be truly human, that they had that thought with them in their last moments to make self-devotion more easy, and death more sweet?

And yet—and yet—is not the highest heroism that which is free even from the approbation of our fellowmen, even from the approbation of the best and wisest? The heroism which is known only to our Father who seeth in secret? The Godlike deeds alone in the lonely chamber? The Godlike lives lived in obscurity?—a heroism rare among us men, who live perforce in the glare and noise of the outer world: more common among women; women of whom the world never hears; who, if the world discovered them, would only draw the veil more closely over their faces and their hearts, and entreat to be left alone with God. True, they cannot always hide. They must not always hide; or their fellow-creatures would lose the golden lesson. But, nevertheless, it is of the essence of the perfect and womanly heroism, in which, as in all spiritual forces the woman transcends the man, that it would hide if it could.

And it was a pleasant thought to me, when I glanced lately at the golden deeds of women in Miss Yonge's book—it was a pleasant thought to me, that I could say to myself—Ah! yes. These heroines are known, and their fame flies through the mouths of men. But if so, how many thousands of heroines there must have been, how many thousands there may be now, of whom we shall never know. But still they are there. They sow in secret the seed of which we pluck the flower and eat the fruit, and know not that we pass the sower daily in the street; perhaps some humble, ill-dressed woman, earning painfully her own small sustenance. She who nurses a bedridden mother, instead of sending her to the workhouse. She who spends her heart and her money on a drunken father, a reckless brother, on the orphans of a kinsman or a friend. She who—But why go on with the long list of great little heroisms, with which a clergyman at least comes in contact daily—and it is one of the most ennobling privileges of a clergyman's high calling that he does come in contact with them—why go on, I say, save to commemorate one more form of great little heroism—the commonest, and yet the least remembered of all—namely, the heroism of an average mother? Ah, when I think of that last broad fact, I gather hope again for poor humanity; and this dark world looks bright, this diseased world looks wholesome to me once more—because, whatever else it is or is not full of, it is at least full of mothers.

While the satirist only sneers, as at a stock butt for his ridicule, at the managing mother trying to get her daughters married off her hands by chicaneries and meannesses, which every novelist knows too well how to draw—would to heaven he, or rather, alas! she would find some more chivalrous employment for his or her pen—for were they not, too, born of woman?—I only say to myself—having had always a secret fondness for poor Rebecca, though I love Esau more than Jacob—Let the poor thing alone. With pain she brought these girls into the world. With pain she educated them according to her light. With pain she is trying to obtain for them the highest earthly blessing of which she can conceive, namely, to be well married; and if in doing that last, she manoeuvres a little, commits a few basenesses, even tells a few untruths, what does all that come to, save this—that in the confused intensity of her motherly self-sacrifice, she will sacrifice for her daughters even her own conscience and her own credit? We may sneer, if we will, at such a poor hard-driven soul when we meet her in society; our duty, both as Christians and ladies and gentlemen, seems to me to be—to do for her something very different indeed.

But to return. Looking at the amount of great little heroisms, which are being, as I assert, enacted around us every day, no one has a right to say, what we are all tempted to say at times: "How can I be heroic? This is no heroic age, setting me heroic examples. We are growing more and more comfortable, frivolous, pleasure-seeking, money-making; more and more utilitarian; more and more mercenary in our politics, in our morals, in our religion; thinking less and less of honour and duty, and more and more of loss and gain. I am born into an unheroic time. You must not ask me to become heroic in it."

I do not deny that it is more difficult to be heroic, while circumstances are unheroic round us. We are all too apt to be the puppets of circumstances; all too apt to follow the fashion; all too apt, like so many minnows, to take our colour from the ground on which we lie, in hopes, like them, of comfortable concealment, lest the new tyrant deity, called Public Opinion, should spy us out, and, like Nebuchadnezzar of old, cast us into a burning fiery furnace—which public opinion can make very hot—for daring to worship any god or man save the will of the temporary majority.

Yes, it is difficult to be anything but poor, mean, insufficient, imperfect people, as like each other as so many sheep; and, like so many sheep, having no will or character of our own, but rushing altogether blindly over the same gap, in foolish fear of the same dog, who, after all, dare not bite us; and so it always was and always will be.

For the third time I say,

Unless above himself he can
Exalt himself, how poor a thing is man.

But, nevertheless, any man or woman who *will*, in any age and under any circumstances, can live the heroic life and exercise heroic influences.

If any ask proof of this, I shall ask them, in return, to read two novels; novels, indeed, but, in their method and their moral, partaking of that heroic and ideal element, which will make them live, I trust, long after thousands of mere novels have returned to their native dust. I mean Miss Muloch's "John Halifax, Gentleman," and Mr. Thackeray's "Esmond," two books which no man or woman ought to read without being the nobler for them.

"John Halifax, Gentleman," is simply the history of a poor young clerk, who rises to be a wealthy mill-owner in the manufacturing districts, in the early part of this century. But he contrives to be an heroic and ideal clerk, and an heroic and ideal mill-owner; and that without doing anything which the world would call heroic or ideal, or in anywise stepping out of his sphere, minding simply his own business, and doing the duty which lies nearest him. And how? By getting into his head from youth the strangest notion, that in whatever station or business he may be, he can always be what he considers a gentleman; and that if he only behaves like a gentleman, all must go right at last. A beautiful book. As I said before, somewhat of an heroic and ideal book. A book which did me good when first I read it; which ought to do any young man good who will read it, and then try to be, like John Halifax, a gentleman, whether in the shop, the counting-house, the bank, or the manufactory.

The other—an even more striking instance of the possibility, at least, of heroism anywhere and everywhere—is Mr. Thackeray's "Esmond." On the meaning of that book I can speak with authority. For my dear and regretted friend told me himself that my interpretation of it was the true one; that this was the lesson which he meant men to learn therefrom.

Esmond is a man of the first half of the eighteenth century; living in a coarse, drunken, ignorant, profligate, and altogether unheroic age. He is—and here the high art and the high morality of Mr. Thackeray's genius is shown—altogether a man of his own age. He is not a sixteenth-century or a nineteenth-century man born out of time. His information, his politics, his religion, are no higher than of those round him. His manners, his views of human life, his very prejudices and faults, are those of his age. The temptations which he conquers are just those under which the men around him fall. But how does he conquer them? By holding fast throughout to honour, duty, virtue. Thus, and thus alone, he becomes an ideal eighteenth-century gentleman, an eighteenth-century hero. This was what Mr. Thackeray meant—for he told me so himself, I say—that it was possible, even in England's lowest and foulest times, to be a gentleman and a hero, if a man would but be true to the light within him.

But I will go farther. I will go from ideal fiction to actual, and yet ideal, fact; and say that, as I read history, the most unheroic age which the civilised world ever saw was also the most heroic; that the spirit of man triumphed most utterly over his circumstances at the very moment when those circumstances were most against him.

How and why he did so is a question for philosophy in the highest sense of that word. The fact of his having done so is matter of history. Shall I solve my own riddle?

Then, have we not heard of the early Christian martyrs? Is there a doubt that they, unlettered men, slaves, weak women, even children, did exhibit, under an infinite sense of duty, issuing in infinite self-sacrifice, a heroism such as the world had never seen before; did raise the ideal of human nobleness a whole stage—rather say, a whole heaven—higher than before; and that wherever the tale of their great deeds spread, men accepted, even if they did not copy, those martyrs as ideal specimens of the human race, till they were actually worshipped by succeeding generations, wrongly, it may be, but pardonably, as a choir of lesser deities?

But is there, on the other hand, a doubt that the age in which they were heroic was the most unheroic of all ages; that they were bred, lived, and died, under the most debasing of materialist tyrannies, with art, literature, philosophy, family and national life dying, or dead around them, and in cities the corruption of which cannot be told for very shame—cities, compared with which Paris is the abode of Arcadian simplicity and innocence? When I read Petronius and Juvenal, and recollect that they were the contemporaries of the Apostles; when—to give an instance which scholars, and perhaps, happily, only scholars, can appreciate—I glance once more at Trimalchio's feast, and remember that within a mile of that feast St. Paul may have been preaching to a Christian congregation, some of whom—for St. Paul makes no secret of that strange fact—may have been, ere their conversion, partakers in just such vulgar and bestial orgies as those which were going on in the rich freedman's halls; after that, I say, I can put no limit to the possibility of man's becoming heroic, even though he be surrounded by a hell on earth; no limit to the capacities of any human being to form for himself or herself a high and pure ideal of human character; and, without "playing fantastic tricks before high heaven," to carry out that ideal in every-day life; and in the most commonplace circumstances, and the most menial occupations, to live worthy of—as I conceive—our heavenly birthright, and to imitate the heroes, who were the kinsmen of the gods.

THE MASSACRE OF THE INNOCENTS [11]

Let me begin by asking the ladies who are interesting themselves in this good work, whether they have really considered what they are about to do in carrying out their own plans? Are they aware that if their Society really succeeds, they will produce a very serious, some would think a very dangerous, change in the state of this nation? Are they aware that they would probably save the lives of some thirty or forty per cent. of the children who are born in England, and that therefore they would cause the subjects of Queen Victoria to increase at a very far more rapid rate than they do now? And are they aware that some very wise men inform us that England is already over-peopled, and that it is an exceedingly puzzling question where we shall soon be able to find work or food for our masses, so rapidly do they increase already, in spite of the thirty or forty per cent. which kind Nature carries off yearly before they are five years old? Have they considered what they are to do with all those children whom they are

11   Speech in behalf of Ladies' Sanitary Association. Delivered at St. James's Hall, London, 1859.

going to save alive? That has to be thought of; and if they really do believe, with some political economists, that over-population is a possibility to a country which has the greatest colonial empire that the world has ever seen; then I think they had better stop in their course, and let the children die, as they have been in the habit of dying.

But if, on the other hand, it seems to them, as I confess it does to me, that the most precious thing in the world is a human being; that the lowest, and poorest, and the most degraded of human beings is better than all the dumb animals in the world; that there is an infinite, priceless capability in that creature, fallen as it may be; a capability of virtue, and of social and industrial use, which, if it is taken in time, may be developed up to a pitch, of which at first sight the child gives no hint whatsoever; if they believe again, that of all races upon earth now, the English race is probably the finest, and that it gives not the slightest sign whatever of exhaustion; that it seems to be on the whole a young race, and to have very great capabilities in it which have not yet been developed, and above all, the most marvellous capability of adapting itself to every sort of climate and every form of life, which any race, except the old Roman, ever has had in the world; if they consider with me that it is worth the while of political economists and social philosophers to look at the map, and see that about four-fifths of the globe cannot be said as yet to be in anywise inhabited or cultivated, or in the state into which men could put it by a fair supply of population, and industry, and human intellect: then, perhaps, they may think with me that it is a duty, one of the noblest of duties, to help the increase of the English race as much as possible, and to see that every child that is born into this great nation of England be developed to the highest pitch to which we can develop him in physical strength and in beauty, as well as in intellect and in virtue. And then, in that light, it does seem to me, that this Institution—small now, but I do hope some day to become great and to become the mother institution of many and valuable children—is one of the noblest, most right-minded, straightforward, and practical conceptions that I have come across for some years.

We all know the difficulties of sanitary legislation. One looks at them at times almost with despair. I have my own reasons, with which I will not trouble this meeting, for looking on them with more despair than ever: not on account of the government of the time, or any possible government that could come to England, but on account of the peculiar class of persons in whom the ownership of the small houses has become more and more vested, and who are becoming more and more, I had almost said, the arbiters of the popular opinion, and of every election of parliament. However, that is no business of ours here; that must be settled somewhere else; and a fearfully long time, it seems to me, it will be before it is settled. But, in the meantime, what legislation cannot do, I believe private help, and, above all, woman's help, can do even better. It can do this; it can improve the condition of the working man: and not only of him; I must speak also of the middle classes, of the men who own the house in which the working man lives. I must speak, too, of the wealthy tradesman; I must speak—it is a sad thing to have to say it—of our own class as well as of others. Sanitary reform, as it is called, or, in plain English, the art of health, is so very recent a discovery, as all true physical science is, that we ourselves and our own class know very little about it, and practise it very little. And this society, I do hope, will bear in mind that it is not simply to seek the working man, not only to go into the foul alley: but it is to go to the door of the farmer, to the door of the shopkeeper, aye, to the door of ladies and gentlemen of the same rank as ourselves. Women can do in that work what men cannot do. The private correspondence, private conversation, private example, of ladies, above all of married women, of mothers of families, may do what no legislation can do. I am struck more and more with the amount of disease and death I see around me in all classes, which no sanitary legislation whatsoever could touch, unless you had a complete house-to-house visitation by some government officer, with powers to enter every dwelling, to drain it, and ventilate it; and not only that, but to regulate the clothes and the diet of every inhabitant, and that among all ranks. I can conceive of nothing short of that, which would be absurd and impossible, and would also be most harmful morally, which would stop the present amount of disease and death which I see around me, without some such private exertion on the part of women, above all of mothers, as I do hope will spring from this institution more and more.

I see this, that three persons out of every four are utterly unaware of the general causes of their own ill-health, and of the ill-health of their children. They talk of their "afflictions," and their "misfortunes;" and, if they be pious people, they talk of "the will of God," and of "the visitation of God." I do not like to trench upon those matters here; but when I read in my book and in your book, "that it is not the will of our Father in Heaven that one of these little ones should perish," it has come to my mind sometimes with very great strength that that may have a physical application as well as a spiritual one; and that the Father in Heaven who does not wish the child's soul to die, may possibly have created that child's body for the purpose of its not dying except in a good old age. For not only in the lower class, but in the middle and upper classes, when one sees an unhealthy family, then in three cases out of four, if one will take time, trouble, and care enough, one can, with the help of the doctor, who has been attending them, run the evil home to a very different cause than the will of God; and that is, to stupid neglect, stupid ignorance, or what is just as bad, stupid indulgence.

Now, I do believe that if those tracts which you are publishing, which I have read and of which I cannot speak too highly, are spread over the length and breadth of the land, and if women—clergymen's wives, the wives of manufacturers and of great employers, district visitors and schoolmistresses, have these books put into their hands, and are persuaded to spread them, and to enforce them, by their own example and by their own counsel—that then, in the course of a few years, this system being thoroughly carried out, you would see a sensible and large increase in the rate of population. When you have saved your children alive, then you must settle what to do with them. But a living dog is better than a dead lion; I would rather have the living child, and let it take its chance, than let it return to God—wasted. O! it is a distressing thing to see children die. God gives the most beautiful and precious thing that earth can have, and we just take it and cast it away; we toss our pearls upon the dunghill and leave them. A dying child is to me one of the most dreadful sights in the world. A dying man, a man dying on the field of battle—that is a small sight; he has taken his chance; he is doing his duty; he has had his excitement; he has had his glory, if that will be any consolation to him; if he is a wise man, he has the feeling that he is dying for his country and his queen: and that is, and ought to be, enough for him. I am not horrified or shocked at the sight of the man who dies on the field of battle; let him die so. It does not horrify or shock me, again, to see a man dying in a good old age, even though the last struggle be painful, as it too often is. But it does shock me, it does make me feel that the world is indeed out of joint, to see a child die. I believe it to be a priceless boon to the child to have lived for a week, or a day: but oh, what has God given to this thankless earth, and what has the earth thrown away; and in nine cases out of ten, from its own neglect and carelessness! What that boy might have been, what he might have done as an Englishman, if he could have lived and grown up healthy and strong! And I entreat you to bear this in mind, that it is not as if our lower or our middle classes were not worth saving: bear in mind that the physical beauty, strength, intellectual power of the middle classes—the shopkeeping class, the farming class, down to the lowest working class— whenever you give them a fair chance, whenever you give them fair food and air, and physical education of any kind, prove them to be the finest race in Europe. Not merely the aristocracy, splendid race as they are, but down and down and down to the lowest labour- ing man, to the navigator—why, there is not such a body of men in Europe as our navigators; and no body of men perhaps have had a worse chance of growing to be what they are; and yet see what they have done! See the magnificent men they become, in spite of all that is against them, dragging them down, tending to give them rickets and consumption, and all the miser- able diseases which children contract; see what men they are, and then conceive what they might be! It has been said, again and again, that there are no more beautiful race of women in Europe than the wives and daughters of our London shopkeepers; and yet there are few races of people who lead a life more in opposition to all rules of hygiene. But, in spite of all that, so wonderful is the vitality of the English race, they are what they are; and therefore we have the finest material to work upon that people ever had. And, therefore, again, we have the less excuse if we do allow English people to grow up puny, stunted, and diseased.

Let me refer again to that word that I used; death— the amount of death. I really believe there are hundreds of good and kind people who would take up this subject with their whole heart and soul if they were aware of the magnitude of the evil. Lord Shaftesbury told you just now that there were one hundred thousand preventable deaths in England every year. So it is. We talk of the loss of human life in war. We are the fools of smoke and noise; because there are cannon-balls, forsooth, and swords and red coats; and because it costs a great deal of money, and makes a great deal of talk in the papers, we think: What so terrible as war? I will tell you what is ten times, and ten thousand times, more terrible than war, and that is outraged Nature. War, we are discovering now, is the clumsiest and most expensive of all games; we are finding that if you wish to commit an act of cruelty and folly, the most costly one that you can commit is to contrive to shoot your fellow-men in war. So it is; and thank God that so it is; but Nature, insidious, inexpensive, silent, sends no roar of cannon, no glitter of arms to do her work; she gives no warning note of preparation; she has no protocols, nor any diplomatic advances, whereby she warns her enemy that war is coming. Silently, I say, and insidiously she goes forth; no! she does not even go forth; she does not step out of her path; but quietly, by the very same means by which she makes alive, she puts to death; and so avenges herself of those who have rebelled against her. By the very same laws by which every blade of grass grows, and every insect springs to life in the sunbeam, she kills, and kills, and kills, and is never tired of killing; till she has taught man the terrible lesson he is so slow to learn, that, Nature is only conquered by obeying her.

And bear in mind one thing more. Man has his courtesies of war, and his chivalries of war; he does not strike the unarmed man; he spares the woman and the child. But Nature is as fierce when she is offended, as she is bounteous and kind when she is obeyed. She spares neither woman nor child. She has no pity; for some awful, but most good reason, she is not allowed to have any pity. Silently she strikes the sleeping babe, with as little remorse as she would strike the strong man, with the spade or the musket in his hand. Ah! would to God that some man had the pictorial eloquence to put before the mothers of England the mass of preventable suffering, the mass of preventable agony of mind and body, which exists in England year after year; and would that some man had the logical eloquence to make them understand that it is in their power, in the power of the mothers and wives of the higher class, I will not say to stop it all—God only knows that—but to stop, as I believe, three-fourths of it.

It is in the power, I believe, of any woman in this room to save three or four lives—human lives—during the next six months. It is in your power, ladies; and it is so easy. You might save several lives apiece, if you choose, without, I believe, interfering with your daily business, or with your daily pleasure; or, if you choose, with your daily frivolities, in any way whatsoever. Let me ask, then, those who are here, and who have not yet laid these things to heart: Will you let this meeting to-day be a mere passing matter of two or three hours' interest, which you may go away and forget for the next book or the next amusement? Or will you be in earnest? Will you learn—I say it openly—from the noble chairman, how easy it is to be in earnest in life; how every one of you, amid all the artificial complications of English society in the nineteenth century, can find a work to do, a noble work to do, a chivalrous work to do—just as chivalrous as if you lived in any old magic land, such as Spenser talked of in his "Faerie Queene;" how you can be as true a knight-errant or lady-errant in the present century, as if you had lived far away in the dark ages of violence and rapine? Will you, I ask, learn this? Will you learn to be in earnest; and to use the position, and the station, and the talent that God has given you to save alive those who should live? And will you remember that it is not the will of your Father that is in Heaven that one little one that plays in the kennel outside should perish, either in body or in soul?

"A MAD WORLD, MY MASTERS." [12]

The cholera, as was to be expected, has reappeared in England again; and England, as was to be expected, has taken no sufficient steps towards meeting it; so that if, as seems but too probable, the plague should spread next summer, we may count with tolerable certainty upon a loss of some ten thousand lives.

That ten thousand, or one thousand, innocent people should die, of whom most, if not all, might be saved alive, would seem at first sight a matter serious enough for the attention of "philanthropists." Those who abhor the practice of hanging one man would, one fancies, abhor equally that of poisoning many; and would protest as earnestly against the painful capital punishment of diarrhoea as against the painless one of hempen rope. Those who demand mercy for the Sepoy, and immunity for the Coolie women of Delhi, unsexed by their own brutal and shameless cruelty, would, one fancies, demand mercy also for the British workman, and immunity for his wife and family. One is therefore somewhat startled at finding that the

12 Fraser's Magazine, No. CCCXXXVII. 1858.

British nation reserves to itself, though it forbids to its armies, the right of putting to death unarmed and unoffending men, women, and children.

After further consideration, however, one finds that there are, as usual, two sides to the question. One is bound, indeed, to believe, even before proof, that there are two sides. It cannot be without good and sufficient reason that the British public remains all but indifferent to sanitary reform; that though the science of epidemics, as a science, has been before the world for more than twenty years, nobody believes in it enough to act upon it, save some few dozen of fanatics, some of whom have (it cannot be denied) a direct pecuniary interest in disturbing what they choose to term the poison-manufactories of free and independent Britons.

Yes; we should surely respect the expressed will and conviction of the most practical of nations, arrived at after the experience of three choleras, stretching over a whole generation. Public opinion has declared against the necessity of sanitary reform: and is not public opinion known to be, in these last days, the Ithuriel's spear which is to unmask and destroy all the follies, superstitions, and cruelties of the universe? The immense majority of the British nation will neither cleanse themselves nor let others cleanse them: and are we not governed by majorities? Are not majorities, confessedly, always in the right, even when smallest, and a show of hands a surer test of truth than any amount of wisdom, learning, or virtue? How much more, then, when a whole free people is arrayed, in the calm magnificence of self-confident conservatism, against a few innovating and perhaps sceptical philosophasters? Then surely, if ever, vox populi is vox coeli.

And, in fact, when we come to examine the first and commonest objection against sanitary reformers, we find it perfectly correct. They are said to be theorists, dreamers of the study, who are ignorant of human nature; and who in their materialist optimism, have forgotten the existence of moral evil till they almost fancy at times that they can set the world right simply by righting its lowest material arrangements. The complaint is perfectly true. They have been ignorant of human nature; they have forgotten the existence of moral evil; and if any religious periodical should complain of their denying original sin, they can only answer that they did in past years fall into that folly, but that subsequent experience has utterly convinced them of the truth of the doctrine.

For, misled by this ignorance of human nature, they expected help, from time to time, from various classes of the community, from whom no help (as they ought to have known at first) is to be gotten. Some, as a fact, expected the assistance of the clergy, and especially of the preachers of those denominations who believe that every human being, by the mere fact of his birth into this world, is destined to endless torture after death, unless the preacher can find an opportunity to deliver him therefrom before he dies. They supposed that to such preachers the mortal lives of men would be in-expressibly precious; that any science which held out a prospect of retarding death in the case of "lost millions" would be hailed as a heavenly boon, and would be carried out with the fervour of men who felt that for the soul's sake no exertion was too great in behalf of the body.

A little more reflection would have quashed their vain hope. They would have recollected that each of these preachers was already connected with a congregation; that he had already a hold on them, and they on him; that he was bound to provide for their spiritual wants before going forth to seek for fresh objects of his ministry. They would have recollected that on the old principle (and a very sound one) of a bird in the hand being worth two in the bush, the minister of a congregation would feel it his duty, as well as his interest, not to defraud his flock of his labours by spending valuable time on a secular subject like sanitary reform, in the hope of possibly preserving a few human beings, whose souls he might hereafter (and that again would be merely a possibility) benefit.

They would have recollected, again, that these congregations are almost exclusively composed of those classes who have little or nothing to fear from epidemics, and (what is even more important) who would have to bear the expenses of sanitary improvements. But so sanguine, so reckless of human conditions had their theories made them, that they actually expected that parish rectors, already burdened with over-work

and vestry quarrels—nay, even that preachers who got
their bread by pew-rents, and whose life-long struggle
was, therefore, to keep those pews filled, and those
renters in good humour—should astound the respectable house-owners and ratepayers who sat beneath
them by the appalling words: "You, and not the 'Visitation of God,' are the cause of epidemics; and of you,
now that you are once fairly warned of your respon-
sibility, will your brothers' blood be required." Conceive Sanitary Reformers expecting this of "ministers,"
let their denomination be what it might—many of the
poor men, too, with a wife and seven children! Truly
has it been said, that nothing is so cruel as the unrea-
sonableness of a fanatic.

They forgot, too, that sanitary science, like geology, must be at first sight "suspect" in the eyes of the
priests of all denominations, at least till they shall
have arrived at a much higher degree of culture than
they now possess.

Like geology, it interferes with that Deus e machina
theory of human affairs which has been in all ages the
stronghold of priestcraft. That the Deity is normally
absent, and not present; that he works on the world
by interference, and not by continuous laws; that it
is the privilege of the priesthood to assign causes for
these "judgments" and "visitations" of the Almighty,
and to tell mankind why He is angry with them, and
has broken the laws of nature to punish them—this,
in every age, has seemed to the majority of priests a
doctrine to be defended at all hazards; for without it,

so they hold, their occupation were gone at once.[13] No wonder, then, if they view with jealousy a set of lay-men attributing these "judgments" to purely chemi-cal laws, and to misdoings and ignorance which have as yet no place in the ecclesiastical catalogue of sins. True, it may be that the Sanitary Reformers are right; but they had rather not think so. And it is very easy not to think so. They only have to ignore, to avoid examining, the facts. Their canon of utility is a pe-culiar one; and with facts which do not come under that canon they have no concern. It may be true, for instance, that the eighteenth century, which to the clergy is a period of scepticism, darkness, and spiri-tual death, is the very century which saw more done for science, for civilisation, for agriculture, for manu-facture, for the prolongation and support of human life than any preceding one for a thousand years and more. What matter? That is a "secular" question, of which they need know nothing. And sanitary reform (if true) is just such another; a matter (as slavery has been seen to be by the preachers of the United States) for the legislator, and not for those whose kingdom is "not of this world."

Others again expected, with equal wisdom, the as-sistance of the political economist. The fact is unde-niable, but at the same time inexplicable. What they could have found in the doctrines of most modern

---

13 We find a most honourable exception to this rule in a sermon by the Rev. C. Richson, of Manchester, on the Sanitary Laws of the Old Testament, with notes by Dr. Sutherland.

political economists which should lead them to suppose that human life would be precious in their eyes, is unknown to the writer of these pages. Those whose bugbear has been over-population, whose motto has been an euphuistic version of

The more the merrier; but the fewer the better fare—

cannot be expected to lend their aid in increasing the population by saving the lives of two-thirds of the children who now die prematurely in our great cities; and so still further overcrowding this unhappy land with those helpless and expensive sources of national poverty—rational human beings, in strength and health.

Moreover—and this point is worthy of serious attention—that school of political economy, which has now reached its full development, has taken all along a view of man's relation to Nature diametrically opposite to that taken by the Sanitary Reformer, or indeed by any other men of science. The Sanitary Reformer holds, in common with the chemist or the engineer, that Nature is to be obeyed only in order to conquer her; that man is to discover the laws of her existing phenomena, in order that he may employ them to create new phenomena himself; to turn the laws which he discovers to his own use; if need be, to counteract one by another. In this power, it has seemed to them, lay his dignity as a rational being. It was this, the power of invention, which made him a progressive animal, not bound as the bird and the bee are, to build exactly as his forefathers built five thousand years ago.

By political economy alone has this faculty been denied to man. In it alone he is not to conquer nature, but simply to obey her. Let her starve him, make him a slave, a bankrupt, or what not, he must submit, as the savage does to the hail and the lightning. "Laissez-faire," says the "Science du neant," the "Science de la misere," as it has truly and bitterly been called; "Laissez-faire." Analyse economic questions if you will: but beyond analysis you shall not step. Any attempt to raise political economy to its synthetic stage is to break the laws of nature, to fight against facts—as if facts were not made to be fought against and conquered, and put out of the way, whensoever they interfere in the least with the welfare of any human being. The drowning man is not to strike out for his life lest by keeping his head above water he interfere with the laws of gravitation. Not that the political economist, or any man, can be true to his own fallacy. He must needs try his hand at the synthetic method though he forbids it to the rest of the world: but the only deductive hint which he has as yet given to mankind is, quaintly enough, the most unnatural "eidolon specus" which ever entered the head of a dehumanised pedant—namely, that once famous "Preventive Check," which, if a nation did ever apply it—as it never will—could issue, as every doctor knows, in nothing less than the questionable habits of abortion, child-murder, and unnatural crime.

The only explanation of such conduct (though one which the men themselves will hardly accept) is this— that they secretly share somewhat in the doubt which many educated men have of the correctness of their inductions; that these same laws of political economy (where they leave the plain and safe subject-matter of trade) have been arrived at somewhat too hastily; that they are, in plain English, not quite sound enough yet to build upon; and that we must wait for a few more facts before we begin any theories. Be it so. At least, these men, in their present temper of mind, are not likely to be very useful to the Sanitary Reformer.

Would that these men, or the clergy, had been the only bruised reed in which the Sanitary Reformers put their trust. They found another reed, however, and that was Public Opinion; but they forgot that (whatever the stump-orators may say about this being the age of electric thought, when truth flashes triumphant from pole to pole, etc.) we have no proof whatsoever that the proportion of fools is less in this generation than in those before it, or that truth, when unpalatable (as it almost always is), travels any faster than it did five hundred years ago. They forgot that every social improvement, and most mechanical ones, have had to make their way against laziness, ignorance, envy, vested wrongs, vested superstitions, and the whole vis inertiae of the world, the flesh, and the devil. They were guilty indeed, in this case, not merely of ignorance of human nature, but of forgetfulness of fact. Did they not know that the excellent New

Poor-law was greeted with the curses of those very farmers and squires who now not only carry it out lovingly and willingly to the very letter, but are often too ready to resist any improvement or relaxation in it which may be proposed by that very Poor-law Board from which it emanated? Did they not know that Agricultural Science, though of sixty years' steady growth, has not yet penetrated into a third of the farms of England; and that hundreds of farmers still dawdle on after the fashion of their forefathers, when by looking over the next hedge into their neighbour's field they might double their produce and their profits? Did they not know that the adaptation of steam to machinery would have progressed just as slowly, had it not been a fact patent to babies that an engine is stronger than a horse; and that if cotton, like wheat and beef, had taken twelve months to manufacture, instead of five minutes, Manchester foresight would probably have been as short and as purblind as that of the British farmer? What right had they to expect a better reception for the facts of Sanitary Science?—facts which ought to, and ultimately will, disturb the vested interests of thousands, will put them to inconvenience, possibly at first to great expense; and yet facts which you can neither see nor handle, but must accept and pay hundreds of thousands of pounds for, on the mere word of a doctor or inspector who gets his living thereby. Poor John Bull! To expect that you would accept such a gospel cheerfully was indeed to expect too much!

But yet, though the public opinion of the mass could not be depended on, there was a body left, distinct from the mass, and priding itself so much on that distinctness that it was ready to say at times—of course in more courteous—at least in what it considered more Scriptural language: "This people which knoweth not the law is accursed." To it therefore—to the religious world—some over-sanguine Sanitary Reformers turned their eyes. They saw in it ready organised (so it professed) for all good works, a body such as the world had never seen before. Where the religions public of Byzantium, Alexandria, or Rome numbered hundreds, that of England numbered its thousands. It was divided, indeed, on minor points, but it was surely united by the one aim of saving every man his own soul, and of professing the deepest reverence for that Divine Book which tells men that the way to attain that aim is, to be good and to do good; and which contains among other commandments this one—"Thou shaft not kill." Its wealth was enormous. It possessed so much political power, that it would have been able to command elections, to compel ministers, to encourage the weak hearts of willing but fearful clergymen by fair hopes of deaneries and bishoprics. Its members were no clique of unpractical fanatics—no men less. Though it might number among them a few martinet ex-post-captains, and noblemen of questionable sanity, capable of no more practical study than that of unfulfilled prophecy, the vast majority of them were landowners, merchants, bankers, commercial men of all ranks, full of worldly experience, and of the science of organisation, skilled all their lives in finding and in employing men and money. What might not be hoped from such a body, to whom that commercial imperium in imperio of the French Protestants which the edict of Nantes destroyed was poor and weak? Add to this that these men's charities were boundless; that they were spending yearly, and on the whole spending wisely and well, ten times as much as ever was spent before in the world, on educational schemes, missionary schemes, church building, reformatories, ragged schools, needlewomen's charities—what not? No object of distress, it seemed, could be discovered, no fresh means of doing good devised, but these men's money poured bountifully and at once into that fresh channel, and an organisation sprang up for the employment of that money, as thrifty and as handy as was to be expected from the money-holding classes of this great commercial nation.

What could not these men do? What were they not bound by their own principles to do? No wonder that some weak men's hearts beat high at the thought. What if the religious world should take up the cause of Sanitary Reform? What if they should hail with joy a cause in which all, whatever their theological differences, might join in one sacred crusade against dirt, degradation, disease, and death? What if they should rise at the hustings to inquire of every candidate: "Will you or will you not, pledge yourself to carry out Sanitary Reform in the place for which you are elected, and let the health and the lives of the local poor be that 'local interest' which you are bound by your election to defend? Do you confess your ignorance of the subject? Then know, sir, that you are unfit, at this point of the nineteenth century, to be a member of the British Senate. You go thither to make laws 'for the preservation of life and property.' You confess yourself ignorant of those physical laws, stronger and wider than any which you can make, upon which all human life depends, by infringing which the whole property of a district is depreciated." Again, what might not the "religious world," and the public opinion of "professing Christians," have done in the last twenty—ay, in the last three years?

What it has done, is too patent to need comment here.

The reasons of so strange an anomaly are to be approached with caution. It is a serious thing to impute motives to a vast body of men, of whom the majority are really respectable, kind-hearted, and useful; and if in giving one's deliberate opinion one seems to blame them, let it be recollected that the blame lies not so much on them as on their teachers: on those who, for some reasons best known to themselves, have truckled to, and even justified, the self-satisfied ignorance of a comfortable moneyed class.

But let it be said, and said boldly, that these men's conduct in the matter of Sanitary Reform seems at least to show that they value virtue, not for itself, but for its future rewards. To the great majority of these men (with some heroic exceptions, whose names may be written in no subscription list, but are surely written in the book of life) the great truth has never been revealed, that good is the one thing to be done, at all risks, for its own sake; that good is absolutely and infinitely better than evil, whether it pay or not to all eternity. Ask one of them: "Is it better to do right and go to hell, or do wrong and go to heaven?"—they will look at you puzzled, half angry, suspecting you of some secret blasphemy, and, if hard pressed, put off the new and startling question by saying, that it is absurd to talk of an impossible hypothesis. The human portion of their virtue is not mercenary, for they are mostly worthy men; the religious part thereof, that which they keep for Sundays and for charitable institutions, is too often mercenary, though they know it not. Their religion is too often one of "Loss and Gain," as much as Father Newman's own; and their actions, whether they shall call them "good works" or "fruits of faith," are so much spiritual capital, to be repaid with interest at the last day.

Therefore, like all religionists, they are most anxious for those schemes of good which seem most profitable to themselves and to the denomination to which they belong; and the best of all such works is, of course, as with all religionists, the making of proselytes. They really care for the bodies, but still they care more for the souls, of those whom they assist—and not wrongly either, were it not that to care for a man's soul usually means, in the religious world, to make him think with you; at least to lay him under such obligations as to give you spiritual power over him. Therefore it is that all religious charities in England are more and more conducted, just as much as those of Jesuits and Oratorians, with an ulterior view of proselytism; therefore it is that the religious world, though it has invented, perhaps, no new method of doing good; though it has been indebted for educational movements, prison visitations, infant schools, ragged schools, and so forth, to Quakers, cobblers, even in some cases to men whom they call infidels, have gladly adopted each and every one of them, as fresh means of enlarging the influence or the numbers of their own denominations, and of baiting for the body in order to catch the soul. A fair sample of too much of their labour may be seen anywhere, in those tracts in which the prettiest stories, with the prettiest binding and pictures, on the most secular—even, sometimes, scientific—of subjects, end by a few words of pious exhortation, inserted by a different hand from that which indites the "carnal" mass of the book. They did not invent the science, or the art of story-telling, or the woodcutting, or the plan of getting books up prettily—or, indeed, the notion of instructing the masses at all; but finding these things in the hands of "the world," they have "spoiled the Egyptians," and fancy themselves beating Satan with his own weapons.

If, indeed, these men claimed boldly all printing, all woodcutting, all story-telling, all human arts and sciences, as gifts from God Himself; and said, as the book which they quote so often says: "The Spirit of God gives man understanding, these, too, are His gifts, sacred, miraculous, to be accounted for to Him," then they would be consistent; and then, too, they would have learnt, perhaps, to claim Sanitary Science for a gift divine as any other: but nothing, alas! is as yet further from their creed. And therefore it is that Sanitary Reform finds so little favour in their eyes. You have so little in it to show for your work. You may think you have saved the lives of hundreds; but you cannot put your finger on one of them: and they know you not; know not even their own danger, much less your beneficence. Therefore, you have no lien on them, not even that of gratitude; you cannot say to a man: "I have prevented you having typhus, therefore you must attend my chapel." No! Sanitary Reform makes no proselytes. It cannot be used as a religious engine. It is too simply human, too little a respecter of persons, too like to the works of Him who causes His sun to shine on the evil and the good, and His rain to fall on the just and on the unjust, and is good to the unthankful and to the evil, to find much favour in the eyes of a generation which will compass sea and land to make one proselyte.

Yes. Too like the works of our Father in heaven, as indeed all truly natural and human science needs must be. True, to those who believe that there is a Father in heaven, this would, one supposes, be the highest recommendation. But how many of this generation believe that? Is not their doctrine, the doctrine to testify for which the religious world exists, the doctrine which if you deny, you are met with one universal frown and snarl—that man has no Father in heaven: but that if he becomes a member of the religious world, by processes varying with each denomination, he may—strange paradox—create a Father for himself?

But so it is. The religious world has lost the belief which even the elder Greeks and Romans had, of a "Zeus, Father of gods and men." Even that it has lost. Therefore have man and the simple human needs of man, no sacredness in their eyes; therefore is Nature to them no longer "the will of God exprest in facts," and to break a law of nature no longer to sin against Him who "looked on all that He had made, and behold, it was very good." And yet they read their Bibles, and believe that they believe in Him who stood by the lake-side in Galilee, and told men that not a sparrow fell to the ground without their Father's knowledge—and that they were of more value than many sparrows. Do those words now seem to some so self-evident as to be needless? They will never seem so to the Sanitary Reformer, who has called on the "British Public" to exert themselves in saving the lives of thousands yearly; and has received practical answers which will furnish many a bitter jest for the Voltaire of the next so-called "age of unbelief," or fill a sad, but an instructive chapter in some future enlarged edition of Adelung's "History of Human Folly."

All but despairing, Sanitary Reformers have turned again and again to her Majesty's Government. Alas for them! The Government was ready and willing enough to help. The wicked world said: "Of course. It will create a new department. It will give them more places to bestow." But the real reason of the willingness of Government seems to be that those who compose it are thoroughly awake to the importance of the subject.

But what can a poor Government do, whose strength consists (as that of all English Governments must) in not seeming too strong; which is allowed to do anything, only on condition of doing the minimum? Of course, a Government is morally bound to keep itself in existence; for is it not bound to believe that it can govern the country better than any other knot of men? But its only chance of self-preservation is to know, with Hesiod's wise man, "how much better the half is than the whole," and to throw over many a measure which it would like to carry, for the sake of saving the few which it can carry.

An English Government, nowadays, is simply at the mercy of the forty or fifty members of the House of Commons who are crotchety enough or dishonest enough to put it unexpectedly in a minority; and they, with the vast majority of the House, are becoming more and more the delegates of that very class which is most opposed to Sanitary Reform. The honourable member goes to Parliament not to express his opinions, (for he has stated most distinctly at the last election that he has no opinions whatsoever), but to protect the local interests of his constituents. And the great majority of those constituents are small houseowners—the poorer portion of the middle class. Were he to support Government in anything like a sweeping measure of Sanitary Reform, woe to his seat at the next election; and he knows it; and therefore, even if he allow the Government to have its Central Board of Health, he will take good care, for his own sake, that the said Board shall not do too much, and that it shall not compel his constituents to do anything at all.

No wonder, that while the attitude of the House of Commons is such toward a matter which involves the lives of thousands yearly, some educated men should be crying that Representative institutions are on their trial, and should sigh for a strong despotism.

There is an answer, nevertheless, to such sentimentalists, and one hopes that people will see the answer for themselves, and that the infection of Imperialism, which seems spreading somewhat rapidly, will be stopped by common sense and honest observation of facts.

A despotism doubtless could carry out Sanitary Reform: but doubtless, also, it would not.

A despot in the nineteenth century knows well how insecure his tenure is. His motto must be, "Let us eat and drink, for to-morrow we die;" and, therefore, the first objects of his rule will be, private luxury and a standing army; while if he engage in public works, for the sake of keeping the populace quiet, they will be certain not to be such as will embroil him with the middle classes, while they will win him no additional favour with the masses, utterly unaware of their necessity. Would the masses of Paris have thanked Louis Napoleon the more if, instead of completing the Tuileries, he had sewered the St. Antoine? All arguments to the contrary are utterly fallacious, which are drawn from ancient despotisms, Roman, Eastern, Peruvian, or other; and for this simple reason, that they had no middle class. If they did work well (which is a question) it was just because they had no middle class— that class, which in a free State is the very life of a nation, and yet which, in a despotism, is sure to be the root of its rottenness. For a despot who finds, as Louis Napoleon has done, a strong middle class already existing, must treat it as he does; he must truckle to it, pander to its basest propensities, seem to make himself its tool, in order that he may make it his. For the sake of his own life, he must do it; and were a despot to govern England tomorrow, we should see that the man who was shrewd enough to have climbed to that bad eminence, would be shrewd enough to know that he could scarcely commit a more suicidal act than, by some despotic measure of Sanitary Reform, to excite the ill-will of all the most covetous, the most stupid, and the most stubborn men in every town of England.

There is another answer, too, to "Imperialists" who talk of Representative institutions being on their trial, and let it be made boldly just now.

It will be time to talk of Representative institutions being good or bad, when the people of England are properly represented.

In the first place, it does seem only fair that the class who suffer most from epidemics should have some little share in the appointment of the men on whose votes extermination of epidemics now mainly depends. But that is too large a question to argue here. Let the Government see to it in the coming session.

Yet how much soever, or how little soever, the suffrage be extended in the direction of the working man, let it be extended, at least in some equal degree, in the direction of the educated man. Few bodies in England now express the opinions of educated men less than does the present House of Commons. It is not chosen by educated men, any more than it is by proletaires. It is not, on an average, composed of educated men; and the many educated men who are in it have, for the most part, to keep their knowledge very much to themselves, for fear of hurting the feelings of "ten-pound Jack," or of the local attorney who looks after Jack's vote. And therefore the House of Commons does not represent public opinion.

For, to enounce with fitting clearness a great but much-forgotten truth, To have an opinion, you must have an opinion.

Strange: but true, and pregnant too. For, from it may be deduced this corollary, that nine-tenths of what is called Public Opinion is no opinion at all; for, on the matters which come under the cognizance of the House of Commons (save where superstition, as in the case of the Sabbath, or the Jew Bill, sets folks thinking—generally on the wrong side), nine people out of ten have no opinion at all; know nothing about the matter, and care less; wherefore, having no opinions to be represented, it is not important whether that nothing be represented or not.

The true public opinion of England is composed of the opinions of the shrewd, honest, practical men in her, whether educated or not; and of such, thank God, there are millions: but it consists also of the opinions of the educated men in her; men who have had leisure and opportunity for study; who have some chance of knowing the future, because they have examined the past; who can compare England with other nations; English creeds, laws, customs, with those of the rest of mankind; who know somewhat of humanity, human progress, human existence; who have been practised in the processes of thought; and who, from study, have formed definite opinions, differing doubtless in infinite variety, but still all founded upon facts, by something like fair and scientific induction.

Till we have this class of men fairly represented in the House of Commons, there is little hope for Sanitary Reform: when it is so represented, we shall have no reason to talk of Representative institutions being on their trial.

And it is one of the few hopeful features of the present time, that an attempt is at last being made to secure for educated men of all professions a fair territorial representation. A memorial to the Government has been presented, appended to which, in very great numbers, are the names of men of note, of all ranks, all shades in politics and religion, all professions—legal, clerical, military, medical, and literary. A list of names representing so much intellect, so much learning, so much acknowledged moderation, so much good work already done and acknowledged by the country, has never, perhaps, been collected for any political purpose; and if their scheme (the details of which are not yet made public) should in anywise succeed, it will do more for the prospects of Sanitary Reform than any forward movement of the quarter of a century.

For if Sanitary Reform, or perhaps any really progressive measure, is to be carried out henceforth, we must go back to something like the old principle of the English constitution, by which intellect, as such, had its proper share in the public councils. During those middle ages when all the intellect and learning was practically possessed by the clergy, they constituted a separate estate of the realm. This was the old plan—the best which could be then devised. After learning became common to the laity, the educated classes were represented more and more only by such clever young men as could be thrust into Parliament by the private patronage of the aristocracy. Since the last Reform Bill, even that supply of talent has been cut off; and the consequence has been, the steady deterioration of our House of Commons toward such a level of mediocrity as shall satisfy the ignorance of the practically electing majority, namely, the tail of the middle class; men who are apt to possess all the failings with few of the virtues of those above them and below them; who have no more intellectual training than the simple working man, and far less than the average shopman, and who yet lose, under the influence of a small competence, that practical training which gives to the working man, made strong by wholesome necessity, chivalry, endurance, courage, and self-restraint; whose business morality is made up of the lowest and narrowest maxims of the commercial world, unbalanced by that public spirit, that political knowledge, that practical energy, that respect for the good opinion of his fellows, which elevate the large employer. On the hustings, of course, this description of the average free and independent elector would be called a calumny; and yet, where is the member of Parliament who will not, in his study, assent to its truth, and confess, that of all men whom he meets, those who least command his respect are those among his constituents to secure whom he takes most trouble; unless, indeed, it be the pettifoggers who manage his election for him?

Whether this is the class to whose public opinion the health and lives of the masses are to be entrusted, is a question which should be settled as soon as possible.

Meanwhile let every man who would awake to the importance of Sanitary questions, do his best to teach and preach, in season and out of season, and to instruct, as far as he can, that public opinion which is as yet but public ignorance. Let him throw, for instance, what weight he has into the "National Association for the Advancement of Social Science." In it he will learn, as well as teach, not only on Sanitary Reforms, but upon those cognate questions which must be considered with it, if it is ever to be carried out.

Indeed, this new "National Association" seems the most hopeful and practical move yet made by the sanitarists. It may be laughed at somewhat at first, as the British Association was; but the world will find after a while that, like the British Association, it can do great things towards moulding public opinion, and compel men to consider certain subjects, simply by accustoming people to hear them mentioned. The Association will not have existed in vain, if it only removes that dull fear and suspicion with which Englishmen are apt to regard a new subject, simply because it is new. But the Association will do far more than that. It has wisely not confined itself to any one branch of Social Science, but taken the subject in all its complexity. To do otherwise would have been to cripple itself. It would have shut out many subjects—Law Reform, for instance—which are necessary adjuncts to any Sanitary scheme; while it would have shut out that very large class of benevolent people who have as yet been devoting their energies to prisons, workhouses, and schools. Such will now have an opportunity of learning that they have been treating the symptoms of social disease rather than the disease itself. They will see that vice is rather the effect than the cause of physical misery, and that the surest mode of attacking it is to improve the physical conditions of the lower classes; to abolish foul air, fouled water, foul lodging, and overcrowded dwellings, in which morality is difficult, and common decency impossible. They will not give up—Heaven forbid that they should give up!—their special good works; but they will surely throw the weight of their names, their talents, their earnestness, into the great central object of preserving human life, as soon as they shall have recognised that prevention is better than cure; and that the simple and one method of prevention is, to give the working man his rights. Water, air, light. A right to these three at least he has. In demanding them, he demands no more than God gives freely to the wild beast of the forest. Till society has given him them, it does him an injustice in demanding of him that he should be a useful member of society. If he is expected to be a man, let him at least be put on a level with the brutes. When the benevolent of the land (and they may be numbered by tens of thousands) shall once have learnt this plain and yet awful truth, a vast upward step will have been gained. Because this new Association will teach it them, during the next ten or twenty years, may God's blessing be on it, and, on the noble old man who presides over it.

Often already has he deserved well of his country; but never better than now, when he has lent his great name and great genius to the object of preserving human life from wholesale destruction by unnecessary poison.

And meanwhile let the Sanitary Reformer work and wait. "Go not after the world," said a wise man, "for if thou stand still long enough the world will come round to thee." And to Sanitary Reform the world will come round at last. Grumbling, scoffing, cursing its benefactors; boasting at last, as usual, that it discovered for itself the very truths which it tried to silence, it will come; and will be glad at last to accept the one sibylline leaf, at the same price at which it might have had the whole. The Sanitary Reformer must make up his mind to see no fruit of his labours, much less thanks or reward. He must die in faith, as St. Paul says all true men die, "not having received the promises;" worn out, perhaps, by ill-paid and unappreciated labour, as that truest-hearted and most unselfish of men, Charles Robert Walsh, died but two years ago. But his works will follow him—not, as the preachers tell us, to heaven—for of what use would they be there, to him or to mankind?—but here, on earth, where he set them, that they might go on in his path, after his example, and prosper and triumph long years after he is dead, when his memory shall be blessed by generations not merely "yet unborn," but who never would have been born at all, had he not inculcated into their unwilling fathers the simplest laws of physical health, decency, life—laws which the wild cat of the wood, burying its own excrement apart from its lair, has learnt by the light of nature; but which neither nature nor God Himself can as yet teach to a selfish, perverse, and hypocritical generation.